FRESH ENCOUNTER

Leader's Manual

Henry T. Blackaby & Claude V. King

LifeWay Press
Nashville, Tennessee

© Copyright 1993 • LifeWay Press

All rights reserved

7200-05

Dewey Decimal Classification: 248.4
Subject Heading: CHRISTIAN LIFE//DISCIPLESHIP

Unless indicated otherwise, Scripture quotations are from The Holy Bible,
New International Version, copyright © 1973, 1978, 1984 by International Bible Society.

Printed in the United States of America

LifeWay Press
127 Ninth Avenue, North
Nashville, Tennessee 37234

Contents

How to Use This Manual 7

Overview of *Fresh Encounter* 8

Getting Ready for a Fresh Encounter with God 14

Needed: Spiritual Leaders 23

A Plumb Line for Shepherds 30

Pastor's Preparation Guide 36

Biblical Foundations for Revival Services 40

Guiding God's People to Return to Him 42

Leading a Testimony Service 48

Continuing Renewal 50
    Body Life Meeting
    Love = Obedience

Guiding a Study of *God's Pattern for Revival
and Spiritual Awakening* 57

Session Plans for *God's Pattern for Revival
and Spiritual Awakening*

    Introductory Session 64

    Session 1: An Overview of God's Pattern 72

    Session 2: God Is on Mission in Our World 79

    Session 3: God's People Tend to Depart 87

    Session 4: God Disciplines His People in Love 97

    Session 5: God Calls His People to Repent 104

    Session 6: God Revives His Repentant People 110

How to Use this Manual

WHO NEEDS THIS MANUAL?

Pastors, worship leaders, and other church leaders who will be working together to discern and follow God's leadership in the *Fresh Encounter* process should have a copy of this manual. Every small-group leader who will guide a group study of *God's Pattern for Revival and Spiritual Awakening* will need a copy.

PASTORS AND WORSHIP LEADERS

Because pastors should lead their churches in this process, pastors should read this entire manual. Worship leaders who help plan worship services will also benefit from reading the entire manual. The manual provides many helps to assist you in the process of guiding your church to experience genuine revival. The Holy Spirit will use God's Word through this manual to help you:

- Prepare yourself and your church for a fresh encounter with God,
- Work with existing leaders in your church to lead *Fresh Encounter* on a churchwide scale,
- Guide small-group leaders as they lead their groups through a study of *God's Pattern for Revival and Spiritual Awakening*,
- Guide your church to stand before God's plumb line and to repent whenever God identifies an area in which you have departed from Him,
- Develop ways to help your church regularly renew fellowship with God.

Pastors, you may want to enlist a facilitator to assist with the many details of this process before God. This person can be a church staff member or a lay person.

FRESH ENCOUNTER FACILITATORS

If your pastor has enlisted you to help facilitate the process of *Fresh Encounter*, you should read the following section on "Getting Ready for a Fresh Encounter with God." If you are working directly with the small-group leaders for *God's Pattern for Revival and Spiritual Awakening*, you also will want to study the section "Guiding a Study of *God's Pattern for Revival and Spiritual Awakening*." Work out the details of other assignments with your pastor. Keep your Bible with you at all times to constantly seek God in His Word.

SMALL-GROUP LEADERS FOR *GOD'S PATTERN FOR REVIVAL AND SPIRITUAL AWAKENING*

If your only responsibility is facilitating a small group as they study *God's Pattern for Revival and Spiritual Awakening*, you can move directly to LM* page 57. You may, however, want to read the rest of this manual to understand how your work contributes to the total church process for *Fresh Encounter*.

---

* Cross-references to page numbers in this *Leader's Manual* will use the following codes to identify the resources being referenced:
- **LM:** *Fresh Encounter Leader's Manual* (this manual)
- **GP:** *God's Pattern for Revival and Spiritual Awakening*
- **PL:** *A Plumb Line for God's People*

Overview of Fresh Encounter

In 1985 a missionary family was assigned by their missions organization to a predominantly Moslem urban center. After decades of work, their denomination had five small churches. Friends asked them to reconsider and go to a place where people were responsive to the gospel. After prayer, they were convinced God was calling them to go to this Moslem city. They did not know how to reach the city for Christ, but they knew God did.

With 14 other believers, they agreed to pray until God showed them how He would reach the city. During one of their all-night prayer meetings, they sensed God said to them, "Let Me tell you why I can't reach this city for Christ. I don't have any clean vessels to work with."

They fell on the dirt floor of their meeting house and wept as they confessed their sins. God began to reveal everything in their lives that hindered His work. As revival began among that small group of believers, they began to speak the Word boldly in the marketplace. They began to tell about the love and power of Jesus. God began to demonstrate His power at work through these clean vessels. During the next three and one-half years, 132,000 people made professions of faith in Jesus Christ. When the family came home for furlough in 1989, 156 churches had been started by the new believers in that urban area.

LIGHT AND DARKNESS

We are living in a most exciting time. God is moving mightily to break down long-standing barriers to the gospel. Modern technology is making it possible to preach the gospel to all nations. People worldwide seem to have a greater spiritual hunger today than at any other time in history, and they are responding to the gospel message in numbers that are hard to believe. Nations once closed to Christian witness are now begging for Bibles and for people to teach them about Jesus. From one perspective, we live in a world filled with opportunity and responsiveness to the gospel.

From a quite different view, our nation seems to be growing darker and darker. Wickedness is rapidly increasing. Evil perversion is multiplying. Actions that once were criminal are becoming fashionable. Moral values seem to have disappeared as everyone does what is right in his own eyes. People, organizations, and even governments are actively opposing Christians, and no one seems to fear God. Our nation is at a point of moral and spiritual crisis.

The fact that we face a growing spiritual darkness in our land indicates that the light is not shining brightly. We should not be surprised at the spiritual darkness, but at the lack of light.

Jesus said that His disciples are the light of the world (see Matt. 5:14-16). When the light of Christ is dimmed by the sins and cares of the world on the lives of God's people, darkness increases. When God's people are clean vessels, the light displayed through them causes darkness to flee.

REVIVAL BEFORE SPIRITUAL AWAKENING

God is looking for holy people through whom He can work to reveal Himself to a watching world. God needs clean vessels—people and churches. "What kind of people ought you to be? You ought to live holy and godly lives as you look forward to the day of God and speed its coming.... Make every effort to be found spotless, blameless and at peace with him" (2 Pet. 3:11-12,14).

According to God's pattern for revival and spiritual awakening, spiritual awakening in the land waits for the repentance and revival of God's people. No one desires spiritual awakening more than God does. In His sovereignty God has chosen to work through His people to bring about world redemption and spiritual awakening. That is why God is so brokenhearted when His people are not what they ought to be. In such times not only do His people miss out on fullness of life, but they also slow down His plan of world redemption.

Because of God's great love for His people and a lost world, God disciplines His people in love until they return to Him. God has issued a promise to His people.

> If my people, who are called by my name,
> will humble themselves and pray and seek
> my face and turn from their wicked ways,
> then will I hear from heaven and will for-
> give their sin and will heal their land.
> –2 Chronicles 7:14

The healing of our nation is waiting for the repentance and revival of God's people.

GOD'S INVITATION

Is your church thirsty for a closer relationship with God? Are you like a desert because of a period of spiritual dryness? Do you sense a desperate need for revival in your church? Do you feel a sense of urgency about the moral decay of the nation? Many spiritual leaders sense that revival is our only hope. We believe God Himself is now in the process of calling His people to return to Him. God is saying:

> [37]"If anyone is thirsty, let him come to me and drink. [38]Whoever believes in me, as the Scripture has said, streams of living water will flow from within him."
> –John 7:37-38

> [1]"Come, all you who are thirsty,
>   come to the waters;
> and you who have no money,
>   come, buy and eat!
> Come, buy wine and milk
>   without money and without cost.
> [2]Why spend money on what is not bread,
>   and your labor on what does not satisfy?
> Listen, listen to me, and eat what is good,
>   and your soul will delight in the richest
>   of fare.
> [3]Give ear and come to me;
>   hear me, that your soul may live.
> I will make an everlasting covenant with
> you, my faithful love promised to David."
> –Isaiah 55:1-3

> The Spirit and the bride say, 'Come!' And let him who hears say, 'Come!' Whoever is thirsty, let him come; and whoever wishes, let him take the free gift of the water of life.
> –Revelation 22:17

> "Come to me, all you who are weary and burdened, and I will give you rest."
> –Matthew 11:28

> 'Return to me, and I will return to you,' says the Lord Almighty.
> –Malachi 3:7

> "Repent, then, and turn to God, so that your sins may be wiped out, that times of refreshing may come from the Lord."
> –Acts 3:19

God stands ready to send genuine revival to His people when they respond to His invitation and approach Him through His Word, in the presence of His Spirit, and willingly repent of sins both individually and corporately (as a group). God is calling us to return to Him. God stands ready to return with His mighty power and presence to forgive, cleanse, heal, and restore His people to a right relationship with Himself.

In working with many pastors and other spiritual leaders, we have come to realize that we know how to repent as individuals far better than as churches or groups. For this reason we have prepared *Fresh Encounter* to help you as a spiritual leader as you guide people to return to God.

THE TARGET GROUP

The primary target group for *Fresh Encounter* is where God has His heart—a local church. This manual targets leaders in a church. The processes for corporate (group) repentance and revival, however, will have application to any group of believers in Jesus Christ. This could include groups like:

- churches
- associations
- families
- regional governing bodies
- committees
- denominations
- auxiliaries
- boards
- institutions
- businesses
- agencies
- parachurch groups
- organizations of missionaries

Fresh Encounter is, however, a process for God's people. It is not designed just for individual study, though it would be helpful for individuals. Neither is it designed for independent use by small groups apart from the larger body. We recommend that a church (or group) study this material together so they can respond to God together.

This *Leader's Manual* is designed for use by:

- pastors
- worship leaders
- church staff
- other group or organizational leaders
- and leaders of small groups who are studying *God's Pattern for Revival and Spiritual Awakening*

THE PASTOR'S ROLE

Pastors should guide the church in a fresh encounter with God. Revivals in the Bible were led by established leaders of God's people. The king, governor, prophet, scribe, or priest led nations in revival. Often national revivals included two or more of these leaders. In Nineveh, the king led his city to repent (see Jonah 3). Jacob led his family to repent. We sense the *Fresh Encounter* processes need to be led by a group's established leader rather than an outside leader.

For this reason, we recommend that pastors lead the *Fresh Encounter* processes in a church setting.

The pastor may want to involve church staff or other leaders in the church to act as a leadership team, but the pastor should provide the primary leadership. He also should lead in discerning when and how to guide the church through *Fresh Encounter*. This may require much prayer by the pastor and people as they seek God's directions for their church.

TWO PROCESSES

Fresh Encounter is a tool God can use to assist and guide churches to help members develop a sense of corporate identity with responsibility before God. Under the guidance of the Holy Spirit, these resources can assist churches to examine themselves by God's Word and return to a right relationship with Him. Many churches today need to go through two processes in order to experience revival. Thus, we have developed *Fresh Encounter* to help with these two processes.

PROCESS 1: UNDERSTANDING GOD'S PATTERN

The first process involves a six-week study of *God's Pattern for Revival and Spiritual Awakening*. This small-group Bible study helps members become aware of God's pattern in Scripture and His requirements for revival. The Holy Spirit will help churches reestablish a corporate identity before God as His people. We recommend that this study be undertaken churchwide. The more people who complete this study, the more likely your church will move together with one heart as they turn to God. This study in a church should be preceded by viewing the video message *An Introduction to Fresh Encounter* which overviews God's pattern for revival and spiritual awakening.

PROCESS 2: RETURNING TO THE LORD

The second process guides churches in corporate worship using *A Plumb Line for God's People*. In Amos 7:7-8 God set a measuring line in the middle of His people to help them see how far they had departed from Him.

> ⁷This is what he showed me: The Lord was standing by a wall that had been built true to plumb, with a plumb line in his hand. ⁸And the Lord asked me, "What do you see, Amos?"
>
> "A plumb line," I replied.
>
> Then the Lord said, "Look, I am setting a plumb line among my people Israel; I will spare them no longer."

Israel had departed far from God and rebelled against His attempts to draw them back to Himself. When God showed His prophet Amos a plumb line, He had already determined to bring destruction on His people.

God's call to revival indicates that His people have departed and need to return. God's people, however, do not always realize they have departed from God's original standards. In our day, God's Word serves as a plumb line to reveal God's ideal for the body of Christ (the churches) and for Christian living. As God's people clearly understand God's standards set forth in the Scripture, the Holy Spirit will bring conviction of sin. Godly sorrow over their sin leads to repentance (see 2 Cor. 7:10).

In *A Plumb Line for God's People*, six video messages focus on some of the most common areas in which God's people depart from Him. When individuals or churches recognize they have departed, they immediately need to repent and return to a right love relationship with God. The messages include:

- God's Standard for the Family
- Religion vs. Reality
- Substitutes for God
- World's Ways vs. Kingdom Ways
- Unholy Living vs. Holy Living
- Broken Relationships vs. Unity in the Body

These six messages have been placed in this order intentionally, but they are not necessarily sequential. A church may begin with the subject area they realize needs to be addressed first. Time should then be allotted for the corporate body to process what *God* is saying and respond by doing whatever *God* requires. Individuals and churches should stay *before God* on one subject as long as necessary for *God* to correct them and restore them to a right relationship with Himself.

RESOURCES FOR *FRESH ENCOUNTER*

The following items are the resources you will need to create an environment for a fresh encounter with God.

An Introduction to Fresh Encounter. This videocassette featuring Henry Blackaby is designed for use in large- and small-group settings to overview God's pattern for revival and spiritual awakening. Viewers are invited to participate in a six-week, small-group study of the book, *God's Pattern for Revival and Spiritual Awakening*. Two formats are provided: a 10-minute overview and a more detailed 40-minute explanation.

God's Pattern for Revival and Spiritual Awakening. This member's book guides participants in a six-week study that examines God's pattern for revival and spiritual awakening from a biblical and historical perspective. Each week individuals study five 15-minute assignments. Small groups meet once each week to discuss what members have learned and how God wants them to respond. Christians develop a renewed sense of identity with the people of God and prepare themselves to respond corporately to God's invitation to revival.

A Plumb Line for God's People Video Messages. Six messages by Henry Blackaby are included on two videocassettes. Each message focuses on one subject area giving God's ideal described in Scripture and ways God's people may have departed from Him. The messages can be used in any order. They include: "God's Standard for the Family," "Religion vs. Reality," "Substitutes for God," "World's Ways vs. Kingdom Ways," "Unholy Living vs. Holy Living," and "Broken Relationships vs. Unity in the Body."

A Plumb Line for God's People. This member's book provides summary statements from each of the six video messages, Scripture texts for each theme, and questions to help individuals and churches examine how they measure up against God's plumb line. In the corporate times of worship, each youth and adult participant should have a copy.

Fresh Encounter Audiocassettes. Twelve messages are included on six cassettes in a vinyl album. The first six messages feature Henry Blackaby and Avery Willis discussing the primary subjects in God's pattern for revival and spiritual awakening. The other six messages are audio versions of *A Plumb Line for God's People Video Messages* featuring Henry Blackaby with Avery Willis as host.

Return to Me : A Fresh Encounter with God Through Song. This congregational songbook with accompaniment supports the messages of *Fresh Encounter.* The book has been compiled by Ron and Patricia Owens and contains several new songs that focus specifically on *Fresh Encounter.* A compact disk and an audiocassette tape are available for personal use.

WARNING!
TO PASTORS AND CHURCH LEADERS

The purpose of *Fresh Encounter* is to guide you and your church to stand before God in a fresh encounter with Him. You can anticipate that God is going to be speaking to His church during this study. The Holy Spirit has the assignment to reveal truth and to convict of sin, righteousness, and judgment. Whenever God speaks, He calls for obedience. Do you want God to speak to your church? Then your church must be prepared to obey Him when He does. To hear the Creator of the universe speak to you and then refuse to obey is a terrible offense to God. He is your Creator. Christ is Head of His church. He has every right to be Lord of your church's life. You need to be prepared to release your church to God!

Do not start this study unless you mean business with God. If the Holy Spirit works through the Word of God and brings you face-to-face with God, you are accountable for the relationship. At that point you either must reject Him or obey Him. To sin in ignorance is one thing, but God judges much more severely those who sin with knowledge of the truth (see Heb. 10:26-31 and 2 Pet. 2:20-21). Jesus asked His followers this penetrating question: "Why do you call me, 'Lord, Lord,' and do not do what I say?" (Luke 6:46).

You will not be able to go through this material without coming to know what God requires for His people to return to Him and become His instruments to reach a lost world. If people work through this study and decide not to obey God, they will be far worse off than before. You will be better off not to take this course than to take it and say no to God's will. You cannot encounter God and say no without becoming hardened in heart. However, *not* to help people in this direction is also serious.

Count both costs. Do not count only the cost if you do study the materials and refuse to obey. Ask God to help you grasp the cost of not returning to Him. What will it cost your church if you refuse to even seek God's directions? What will happen if you fail to experience revival?

JEREMIAH AND ISRAEL

Jeremiah 41–42 has the account of a tragic story from Israel's history. Jerusalem had just fallen to the Babylonians. The leaders gathered a remnant of the people and began a journey to Egypt to escape the Babylonians. On the way they decided to seek God's counsel.

> ¹Then all the army officers . . . and all the people from the least to the greatest approached ²Jeremiah the prophet and said to him, "Please hear our petition and pray to the Lord your God for this entire remnant. . . . ³Pray that the Lord your God will tell us where we should go and what we should do."
>
> ⁴"I have heard you," replied Jeremiah the

prophet. "I will certainly pray to the Lord your God as you have requested; I will tell you everything the Lord says and will keep nothing back from you."

⁵Then they said to Jeremiah, "May the Lord be a true and faithful witness against us if we do not act in accordance with everything the Lord your God sends you to tell us. ⁶Whether it is favorable or unfavorable, we will obey the Lord our God."
–Jeremiah 42:1-6

The people took an oath to obey whatever God directed. After ten days the Lord sent word that the people were to stay in the land He had given them. God also sent this warning:

> ¹⁵"If you are determined to go to Egypt and you do go to settle there, ¹⁶then the sword you fear will overtake you there, and the famine you dread will follow you into Egypt, and there you will die."
> –Jeremiah 42:15-16

God knew the hearts of the people were bent on going their own way. They went through the motions of seeking God's directions, but they had already made up their minds to go to Egypt. Jeremiah gave a warning to the people.

> ¹⁹"I warn you today ²⁰that you made a fatal mistake when you sent me to the Lord your God and said, 'Pray to the Lord our God for us; tell us everything he says and we will do it.' ²¹I have told you today, but you still have not obeyed the Lord your God in all he sent me to tell you. ²²So now, be sure of this: You will die by the sword, famine and plague in the place where you want to go to settle."
> –Jeremiah 42:19-22

The people sought God's directions, but they did not intend to change their own plans. According to Jeremiah, that was a fatal mistake that would cost their lives in Egypt.

Studying *Fresh Encounter* will bring you and your people face-to-face with God's requirements for revival in His Word. The Holy Spirit will be teaching you. Be sure you are prepared to lead your people to do whatever God requires. Remember, God will respond to you based on your actions, not on your words alone.

SOME POSSIBLE NEGATIVE REACTIONS

Not everyone will respond positively to *Fresh Encounter*. Scripture is our guide to know how God relates to His people. Scripture also reveals our sin and rebelliousness. Here are some responses you may observe and need to lovingly confront.

1. Some may discount the truth from the Old Testament saying, "God is not like that any more." God, however, does not change. God of the Old Testament is the same God of the New Testament. The Scriptures from Genesis to Revelation reveal Him and the ways He relates to His people. God says, "I the Lord do not change" (Mal. 3:6). James 1:17 says that the "Father of the heavenly lights [the Creator] does not change." Jesus and the writers of the New Testament relied heavily on the Old Testament for instruction. The New Testament church did not have any other Scriptures than the Old Testament. Remember:

> ¹⁶All Scripture is God-breathed and is useful for teaching, rebuking, correcting and training in righteousness, ¹⁷so that the man of God may be thoroughly equipped for every good work.
> –2 Timothy 3:16-17

2. Some are offended to think of God as a God of discipline and judgment. They choose to focus only on God's love and mercy. They try to exert positive thinking hoping to bring about a positive result. In Scripture, God condemned those who went about saying, "Peace, peace" when there was no peace (Jer. 6:14). In the middle of a sinful church, some will say, "We are a great church. Nothing is wrong." God said through Jeremiah, "The prophet who prophesies peace will be recognized as one truly sent by the Lord only if his prediction comes true" (Jer. 28:9). You can use that same criteria and trust that the Holy Spirit will be at work convincing the members of the body of any sin that is present. You may want to use Hebrews 12:1-17 to help them.

3. Some will refuse to deal openly with sin (both past and present) in the church. To protect the church's or a person's reputation, some will disobey the clear teaching of God on how to deal with sin in the church. They prefer to forget about the past and move forward. Open sin that we harbor and refuse to deal with in God's way is sure to shut down God's activity in a church. If we regard iniquity in our hearts, God refuses even to hear our prayers (see Ps. 66:18).

Such a light treatment of sin by some can lead to open rebellion by others. Sin can spread like a fast-growing cancer if not severely dealt with in repentance. Sometimes God requires that sin be dealt with openly in a congregation. To cover up such sins is corporate rebellion by a church.

4. Some will choose to rely on human wisdom and reason even when these are in direct opposition to God's Word. These people may be vocal and forceful. They may present their case in such a way that they say, "Anyone who disagrees with me is a fool." They may argue against God's ways even when confronted with a clear word from Scripture. Do not allow this to keep you or your church from following what God says in His Word. A church and its leaders need to fear God and not fear people. "Let God be true, and every man a liar" (Rom. 3:4). God is far more concerned about your people than you are! Trust God to guide you to know what to say and how to say it. Watch patiently how God moves in your church, in love, to bring His people to a deeper relationship to Himself. Pray for boldness and courage, as the early church did, and it will be given.

NOTES

Getting Ready for a Fresh Encounter with God

> The following information should be read by all leaders related to the *Fresh Encounter* process. Though many of the actions will be taken by the pastor or a primary leader, all leaders will benefit from understanding the process and how each person's work relates to the total process.

Because revival is such a vital need in our churches and in our nation, you may sense an urgency to prepare yourself and your church for using *Fresh Encounter* resources. To get a concentrated period of time to let God speak to you as a spiritual leader, you may want to plan a personal retreat to study and pray through the portions of God's Word suggested in these resources.

Consider a group retreat if the church staff, deacons, elders, church council, or others will be processing this material with you. Such a retreat should allow ample time for individual and group prayer. You may want to designate a period of time for fasting and prayer as you seek God's guidance together.

PASTOR'S (OR PRIMARY LEADER'S) CHECKLIST

The following checklist is a summary of the items discussed in this section. This list can guide you in your study and preparation. If you are going to enlist a staff person or another leader to help you with the details of coordinating *Fresh Encounter*, you will want to work through this process together.

- ❏ 1. Pray that the Lord clearly will guide you to discern His will and timing about the use of *Fresh Encounter* in your church.
- ❏ 2. Enlist some intercessors to pray for you during this preparation phase.
- ❏ 3. Watch *An Introduction to Fresh Encounter* (video).
- ❏ 4. Study *God's Pattern for Revival and Spiritual Awakening* individually or with key leaders in your church.
- ❏ 5. Read the following sections of this manual:
  - ❏ Overview of *Fresh Encounter*
  - ❏ Warning
  - ❏ Needed: Spiritual Leaders
  - ❏ How to Use This Manual
  - ❏ Getting Ready for a *Fresh Encounter* with God
  - ❏ Guiding a Study of *God's Pattern for Revival and Spiritual Awakening*
  - ❏ Session Plans for *God's Pattern for Revival and Spiritual Awakening*
  - ❏ Pastor's Preparation Guide
  - ❏ Guiding God's People to Return to Him
  - ❏ Continuing Renewal
- ❏ 6. Watch *A Plumb Line for God's People* (video).
- ❏ 7. Study *A Plumb Line for God's People* (book).
- ❏ 8. Pray and plan with key leaders ways your church will use the resources to encounter God and respond to Him.
  - ❏ Consider choosing a person as *Fresh Encounter* facilitator.
  - ❏ Introduce *Fresh Encounter* using the introductory videotape.
  - ❏ Determine the time and place for small-group studies.
  - ❏ Decide on when and how to use the *Plumb Line* messages in corporate worship.
  - ❏ Decide on how *Fresh Encounter* will be funded.
  - ❏ Order resources.
  - ❏ Secure needed video equipment.

- ❏ 9. Clear the calendar. Remember, it is God you are seeking with all your heart.
- ❏ 10. Enlist and provide orientation for small-group leaders.
- ❏ 11. Schedule and plan for leadership team meetings.
- ❏ 12. Prepare the people for a fresh encounter with God.
- ❏ 13. Plan for regular times of renewal.
- ❏ 14. Prepare for spiritual awakening.
- ❏ 15. Introduce *God's Pattern for Revival and Spiritual Awakening*.
- ❏ 16. Provide the small-group leaders with copies of the worksheets needed for the study of *God's Pattern for Revival and Spiritual Awakening*.

1. Pray for God's Timing

Not every church or group is at the same place in God's work with them. Please do not treat *Fresh Encounter* as just another program. *Fresh Encounter* is a tool God can use. God alone should be your guide in this process. God alone knows what He wants to do in your church. You need to allow God to guide you according to His purposes and on His timetable. Therefore, pray diligently for God's directions.

God may not want you to use *Fresh Encounter* at this time. If that is the case, don't use it. Don't try to make something happen out of your human desires or effort. God may need some time to further prepare your people for *Fresh Encounter*. He may lead some churches to begin with a study of *Experiencing God: Knowing and Doing the Will of God* (overviewed on *God's Pattern for Revival and Spiritual Awakening*, p. 98) before they move into the *Fresh Encounter* process.

A church might find it beneficial to work through *Step by Step Through the Old Testament* by Waylon Bailey and Tom Hudson, and *Step by Step Through the New Testament* by Thomas D. Lea and Tom Hudson while preparation is being made for *Fresh Encounter*.

God may direct you and your church to deepen your prayer life before you experience *Fresh Encounter*. *Watchman Prayer Ministry* resources can be used by God to link His people in prayer for spiritual awakening. *Disciple's Prayer Life: Walking in Fellowship with God* by T.W. Hunt and Catherine Walker can be used by God to help His people strengthen their prayer life.

Waiting for the Lord requires patience, but when the Lord comes He may move swiftly to accomplish His purposes. Give Him all the time He wants to prepare and refine your church.

Some churches may be in such a time of crisis that an emergency session needs to be called for immediate response to the Lord (see Joel 1–2). Let God direct you and other spiritual leaders in your church concerning whether He wants you to use *Fresh Encounter*, and if so, when.

2. Enlist Prayer Intercessors

This preparation phase requires significant decisions that could lead to genuine revival and spiritual awakening in your church and community. You are absolutely dependent on God to work. Enlist people in your church who are committed and experienced intercessors to pray for you and the other leaders during this time of preparation and throughout the *Fresh Encounter* process.

You may want to give serious consideration to enlisting homebound members as intercessors. They, too, are part of the body of Christ; they may have a wealth of time to devote to prayer. They also need an opportunity for significant service. Call them to action! (See "Starting a Homebound Prayer Force" in *The Church Prayer Ministry Manual* edited by T. W. Hunt, LifeWay Press, 1993, pp. 46–48 for more details about a homebound prayer ministry.)

Provide your intercessors with a specific prayer list. Mention your concerns, decisions to be made, leaders who are involved, meetings for which they can pray, and issues that you anticipate. As prayers are answered, be sure to tell the intercessors so they can rejoice.

As you begin the study of *God's Pattern for Revival and Spiritual Awakening* and the use of *A Plumb Line for God's People*, keep the intercessors informed about specific ways they can pray. Encourage them to stand in the gap (see Ezek. 22:30-31) for your church. Ask them to pray for one more year of God's grace as your church returns to the Lord (see Luke 13:6-9).

3. Watch *An Introduction to Fresh Encounter*

The introductory video will give you an overview of God's pattern for revival and spiritual awakening. You may want initially to watch it twice: once to hear the message and a second time to think about how you will use it in your church.

4. **Study *God's Pattern for Revival and Spiritual Awakening***

The first part of the *Fresh Encounter* process will help you gain an understanding of God's pattern for revival and spiritual awakening. The member's book will help you come to that understanding and help you discern where your church is in God's pattern. You may want to go through this initial study in one of the following ways:

- Study the material by yourself and guide the church as God leads you.
- Study the material with the church staff, deacons, elders, church council, and/or another group of key leaders in the church. Several leaders frequently were used in the biblical revivals. Often greater wisdom comes in the multitude of counselors. Pray with these leaders until you sense God has given clear direction about the next step.
- Study the material with a group of fellow pastors in the community and help one another discern God's directions.

5. **Read this *Fresh Encounter Leader's Manual***

You are already well along in the process of reading this manual. Pastors and worship leaders should read the entire manual. See "How to Use this Manual" (LM p. 7) for other suggestions. Pastors should take time to work through the "Pastor's Preparation Guide" (LM pp. 36).

6. **Watch *A Plumb Line for God's People* Video Messages**

These six video messages have been designed to help your people understand God's plumb line in six major areas. Watch the video to become acquainted with this tool. You will benefit most if you work through the booklet that goes with the video. One unit is covered in each of the video messages.

Pray that God will guide you to know how to best use the messages. You will receive more specific suggestions in the section "Guiding God's People to Return to Him" on LM page 42. Some pastors may choose to preach their own series of messages on these or other topics. That is fine and even encouraged. If you would like to do this, you may want to watch the video as a model of how you can establish clearly God's plumb line for His people.

7. **Study *A Plumb Line for God's People***

Study *A Plumb Line for God's People* one unit at a time as you view the corresponding video message. As you study, you may want to write down questions you think will arise from your people. Again,

be listening to the Lord about when and how to use these messages in your church. Let Him be your guide.

8. **Pray and Plan with Key Leaders**

The pastor should determine which other leaders in the church need to be involved in the decision making process. This could be church staff, deacons or elders, the church council or board, or other key lay leaders. This group should pray together and seek God's directions for the *Fresh Encounter* process. The following are items you may want to consider.

a. **Consider choosing a person as *Fresh Encounter* facilitator.** Though the pastor needs to be the primary person guiding the *Fresh Encounter* process in the church, many details could be handled by a lay person or a member of the church staff. This facilitator could assume responsibility for securing equipment and resources, getting people involved, keeping the church family informed, and so forth.

b. **Introduce *Fresh Encounter* using the videotape *An Introduction to Fresh Encounter*.** Plan to show the longer, detailed segment on God's pattern for revival and spiritual awakening in a worship service where a majority of your people will be in attendance. Their response to God's message on the video should include (1) a time of prayer for God's guidance, and (2) an opportunity to make a commitment to the small-group study of *God's Pattern for Revival and Spiritual Awakening*. At the end of the service or at the beginning of the first small-group session, distribute copies of the member's book.

c. **Determine the time and place for small-group studies.** The best use of *Fresh Encounter* will involve as many members as possible. Because of the serious condition of our churches, this may be a time when major adjustments need to be made. The congregation should study *God's Pattern for Revival and Spiritual Awakening* in small groups of six to ten people. They will need a minimum of one hour each week for group study. Some will need to spend more time each week and/or to extend the number of weeks of the study. Leaders will can monitor the needs of the groups to discern whether adjustments need to be made. Because this is an encounter with God, it may be wise not to try fitting this into a definite number of weeks. God is sovereign! God must have the freedom to guide His people to Himself.

Here are some options for times to meet,

though you may come up with another one that is right for your church.
- Sunday morning during the Sunday School hour using existing leadership for adults and youth
- Sunday afternoon or evening
- Specially called sessions at night or during the day each week

Because this material will challenge your people and require time for meditation and application, we do not recommend that you attempt this part of the study in a retreat setting. People will need time between sessions to pray, study, and apply God's Word to their lives.

Because each unit of study builds on the previous unit or units, newcomers to these groups could consume much time by asking questions. They may feel awkward and unprepared in the groups that have been started. Make preparation for a group that will accommodate all newcomers after the first or second session. Here are some options: (1) Provide small groups that will begin with the Introductory Session and continue beyond the ending time of the other groups. (2) Using more of a lecture method, give a quick overview of the sessions up to the current point; then form new groups of these newcomers who will start the study from that point forward. (3) Provide a group that primarily uses a lecture/discussion method of presentation for the remainder of the sessions.

d. **Decide on when and how to use the *Plumb Line* messages in corporate worship.** The second part of the *Fresh Encounter* process involves returning to God. The *Plumb Line* messages are designed to help individuals and the church identify areas where they may have departed from the Lord. These messages are intended for use in corporate worship. Once the Holy Spirit convicts of sin, individuals and the church need to repent and return to God. Allow time in the service for the video message; for processing the corresponding materials in the member's booklet; and for responding to God during times of prayer, confession, testimony, and invitation. The pastor and other worship leaders should guide these times.

The decision about when and how to use these messages must be God-given. Trust God to guide your church. You may want to pray about these options:
- Study *God's Pattern for Revival and Spiritual Awakening*. Then select one *Plumb Line* message and spend time on that subject before God until you sense God has finished reviving His church in that area. Move to other messages as God directs with an open-ended schedule.
- Study *God's Pattern for Revival and Spiritual Awakening*. Then use one *Plumb Line* message each week for the next six weeks. Watch carefully for the activity of God in His people and respond accordingly.
- Study *God's Pattern for Revival and Spiritual Awakening* prior to a scheduled week of "revival" services. Then use the six *Plumb Line* messages and *A Plumb Line for God's People* member's booklet for six services during the scheduled "revival." The pastor would guide these services. Once genuine revival comes to your church, you will be ready to move your focus to winning the lost to Christ. God may be so moving, this could continue for several weeks!
- Integrate the study of *God's Pattern for Revival and Spiritual Awakening* and the *Plumb Line* messages. Small groups would study a unit from *God's Pattern for Revival and Spiritual Awakening*. Then a corporate worship time would focus on one of the *Plumb Line* messages. The messages are ordered so that the following integration could be followed:

Week 1
God's Pattern: An Overview of God's Pattern (Unit 1)
Plumb Line: God's Standard for the Family

Week 2
God's Pattern: God Is on Mission in Our World (Unit 2)
Plumb Line: Religion vs. Reality

Week 3
God's Pattern: God's People Tend to Depart (Unit 3)
Plumb Line: Substitutes for God

Week 4
God's Pattern: God Disciplines His People in Love (Unit 4)
Plumb Line: World's Ways vs. Kingdom Ways

Week 5
God's Pattern: God Calls His People to Repent (Unit 5)
Plumb Line: Unholy Living vs. Holy Living

Week 6
God's Pattern: God Revives His Repentant People (Unit 6)
Plumb Line: Broken Relationships vs. Unity in the Body

- Study *God's Pattern for Revival and Spiritual Awakening.* Then call the church together for a full weekend of prayer and fasting. Use selected *Plumb Line* messages throughout the weekend. Be aware that God may not be able to accomplish all that He needs to accomplish with His people in only one weekend.

e. **Decide on a funding method.** Some churches may struggle more than others with the cost of providing the resources for this study. Remember that God is your provider. If this is something God is planning for your church, you can trust Him to provide. Again, prayer needs to be a vital part of your work. Ask the church to pray about *Fresh Encounter* and tell them the financial needs. Don't hesitate to give God's people an opportunity to give above their tithe. The key is to trust God to persuade people to give. You need only to make known the need and pray. Watch to see how God will be your provider.

Your church may decide to provide the resources through the church budget, or you may want to ask people to contribute toward the purchase of their own resources.

f. **See that resources are ordered.** Here are the resources you will need:
- *Fresh Encounter Leader's Kit* (7700-01). The kit includes one of each resource in the series including printed resources, videocassettes, and audiocassettes. One kit per church should be sufficient for the pastor or primary leader. If you choose, you may purchase the items separately.
- *Fresh Encounter Introductory Video* (7700-02). Depending on how you introduce the study, you may want to have multiple copies of the introductory video. In most cases, one will be sufficient.
- *Fresh Encounter Leader's Manual* (7200-05). Each key leader will need a copy of this manual. Each small-group leader for *God's Pattern for Revival and Spiritual Awakening* will need a copy.
- *Fresh Encounter: God's Pattern for Revival and Spiritual Awakening* (7200-04). Each youth and adult member involved in the small-group study will need a copy.
- *Fresh Encounter: A Plumb Line for God's People* (7200-03). This booklet will be used with the video messages.during the corporate worship times Each youth and adult will need a copy of the booklet for their personal responses.
- *Fresh Encounter: A Plumb Line for God's People Video Messages* (7700-04). You will need only one set for your church to use in corporate worship.
- *Fresh Encounter Audiocassettes* (7700-03). This optional resource include a total of twelve messages: six messages cover the six units in *God's Pattern for Revival and Spiritual Awakening;* six messages are audio versions of the *Plumb Line* video messages. They will be helpful to leaders. Some people may want to purchase or borrow a set for personal listening. If some people you know have difficulty reading, the audio messages related to *God's Pattern for Revival and Spiritual Awakening* may be helpful for them. You may want to make one or more sets available in the church media library.
- *Return to Me: A Fresh Encounter with God Through Song* (7200-16). This songbook is optional, but it is a valuable asset to the corporate worship experiences as your people respond to God. There is also a compact disk (7700-17) and an audiocassette tape (7700-18) available for personal use. Make members aware of these resources God can use in personal times with Him.

These resources are available by calling 1-800-458-2772. Western states call 1-800-677-7797. You may also write Customer Service Center; 127 Ninth Avenue, North; Nashville, Tennessee 37234; or contact your local Christian bookstore.

g. **Secure needed video equipment.** You will need a VCR and monitor for showing the introductory video and the *Plumb Line* messages. Technicians recommend a monitor for each 25 people. Consider using a large-screen projection video for congregational settings.

9. Clear the Calendar

Activity, even religious activity, can crowd God out of people's lives. Members need to focus their attention on God and His call for their lives. Satan will be happy to use every distraction to keep Christians from dealing with the sin in their lives and churches. Do everything you can as a church to remove any activities that will distract your people from a fresh encounter with God.

A church in Austin, Texas, sensed that God was calling them to repent for a variety of sins. The church decided these actions were far too important to squeeze into a busy church schedule. The leaders decided to cancel all unrelated church programming for the summer months and devote time to prayer, fasting, and repentance.

They had two things on the calendar each week: Sunday morning services and a Wednesday evening church assembly. They spent Wednesday evenings standing before God's Word with a focus on one theme or subject each week. After a time of reading the Word and some brief exposition by the pastor, the people responded to God in prayer, confession, and repentance. They spent the entire summer returning to God.

God did some wonderful things in the lives of individuals, families, and the church. By summer's end, the leaders sensed God was saying to them, "I'm not finished with you yet, but you may return to your regular schedule now."

God may not call you and your church to this kind of radical change in schedule. But for some, completely rearranging schedules may be exactly what God requires. As church leaders, you will have to determine how important revival is for your church. There is a cost to pay for revival. Your church's willingness to make adjustments may be a good indication of how serious you are about genuine revival. Be patient with God's people and trust the Holy Spirit to convince and guide them.

You will be wise to clear the church calendar of as many conflicting events as possible. Because members will be asked to study at home, you will want to keep from competing for their time during the week also. Carefully pray for God's direction regarding your church schedule during the *Fresh Encounter* process.

10. Enlist and Provide an Orientation for Small-Group Leaders

You may use existing small-group leaders to guide the study of *God's Pattern for Revival and Spiritual Awakening*. If you schedule the study when leaders are not already in place, pray that God will call leaders for your groups. Be sensitive to God's leadership as you select leaders.

The learning activities for *God's Pattern for Revival and Spiritual Awakening* are designed to be led by a "lead learner." These leaders do not have to be content experts. They do need to be spiritually mature, and they need skill in leading small-group learning activities. The section "Guiding a Study of *God's Pattern for Revival and Spiritual Awakening*" (LM p. 57) should help them in preparing for and guiding meaningful study sessions. The primary training needed will be an orientation to the materials and the process your church plans to follow. You may choose to guide the leaders through *God's Pattern for Revival and Spiritual Awakening* in small-groups before their leading sessions.

Provide each leader with a copy of *Fresh Encounter Leader's Manual* and *Fresh Encounter: God's Pattern for Revival and Spiritual Awakening*. Ask leaders to read "Guiding a Study of *God's Pattern for Revival and Spiritual Awakening*" in the *Leader's Manual* (LM p. 57) and the introductory material in the member's book through GP page 12 before the orientation.

Adapt and follow the plans for the introductory session (LM p. 64) as an orientation for small-group leaders. Use the *Fresh Encounter Introductory Video* if it is available. In the session, discuss additional details about the church process for *Fresh Encounter* and how the study of *God's Pattern for Revival and Spiritual Awakening* fits into the process. Answer any questions leaders may have. Share plans about leadership team meetings and ask leaders to reserve the dates for those meetings. Explain how you plan to make the needed worksheets available for use in the small groups (see number 16, LM p. 22).

11. Schedule and Plan for Leadership Team Meetings

This study may raise many questions, concerns, and perhaps even problems that will challenge leaders. We recommend you schedule a leadership team meeting every week or every other week to talk about these issues. The meetings should focus on sharing what God seems to be saying to church members, testifying about what God is doing in lives, and discussing questions or problems that have arisen.

This also is a time for group leaders to share with the pastor and church leaders any corporate sins of which members have become aware during their study. These should be prayerfully considered by church leaders. If church leaders sense that your church has sinned in these ways, prayerfully consider how to deal with those sins as a church body. Helps will be provided for this in the section, "Guiding God's People to Return to Him" (LM p. 42).

Devote a significant portion of the leadership team meetings to praying for each other, your pastor, other key church leaders, and the church. The prayer times may well be the most important part of these meetings, so do not cut them short.

12. Prepare the People for a Fresh Encounter with God

The pastor needs to begin preparing the people for a fresh encounter with God. If you are a pastor, allow God to prepare your own heart for revival. Sharing from your own fresh encounter with God may be the best preparation for His people. Personal testimony can spark revival.

Jesus often said that every word He spoke was not His but the Father's. For example, Jesus said, "I did not speak of my own accord, but the Father who sent me commanded me what to say and how to say it. . . . So whatever I say is just what the Father has told me to say" (John 12:49-50). When Jesus said it, it was so. Is that your pattern of ministry? As a spiritual leader, you need to be so intimate with God that when you speak, the people know they have heard a word from God. Your people don't need plain sermons; they need a word from God.

As you and your people study *God's Pattern for Revival and Spiritual Awakening* together, God will be speaking to you. Messages related to the topics being studied will help reinforce God's message to His people. They will help your people make specific application to their lives, their families, and the church.

You may need to teach your people how to respond to God as a corporate body. For instance, they need to know guidelines for confession—when it should be private and when it should be public. Members need to know how to confess moral failure without damaging others and without causing lustful or sinful thoughts to be aroused by the confession. They need to know how to share a life message about what God is doing in their lives in such a way that God gets glory. Helps on page 48 can be used. You may want to spend some time teaching your people how to deal with these subjects before using the *Plumb Line* messages.

Here is a list of things you may want to deal with in preparing your people for a fresh encounter with God.

- Preach about revivals in Scripture.
- Teach about fasting and prayer.
- Discuss the need to quit clock watching when in God's presence.
- Explain how to prepare to meet God. In Exodus 19:9-15 Moses told people to spend two days cleaning up to prepare to meet God. People need clean hands and pure hearts to enter God's presence. Luke 3:2-18 is also a helpful passage. (See "Prepare the Way of the Lord" on GP pp. 94-95 for more help.)
- Focus people's attention on the nature of God and how He works with His people, especially how to know when He is speaking to them personally and corporately.
- Point people to an intimate, real, personal love relationship with God.
- Pray for the demolishing of strongholds due to bondage to the past (see 2 Cor. 10:3-5).
- Help people recognize the difference between spiritual warfare and God's discipline.
- Teach believers to deny self.
- Help believers develop a servant heart for others.
- Teach believers to fear God and to fear offending Him.
- Help believers make an absolute surrender to the lordship of Christ.
- Develop a readiness to release everything to God for reordering: resources, schedule, programs, positions of leadership, calendar of activities, conflicting involvement in secular pursuits, plans, goals, and so forth.
- Prepare for brokenness before restoration. J. Edwin Orr said, "Revival is like judgment day." Help believers understand the process of moving toward spiritual health.
- Help your church look beyond the brokenness to the joy of revival.
- Help believers understand the nature of repentance, personal and corporate.
- Trust God to guide you individually and together as His church.

13. Plan for Regular Times of Renewal

One of the reasons many churches are so far from what God intends is that God's people have failed to renew regularly the love relationship with Him. We may have made attempts at renewal or gone through the motions of revival services, but the current state indicates failure somewhere along the way.

Years ago revival services lasted two or more weeks. The first week was devoted to helping God's people return to the Lord. The second week was devoted to an evangelistic thrust toward the lost. This is the same pattern discussed in *God's Pattern for Revival and Spiritual Awakening*. Revival of God's people must come first. Over the years, however, churches have shortened revival services. Now many devote only three or four days to revivals.

Because of their commitment to reach the lost, churches often have placed the primary emphasis of revival services on evangelistic messages to the lost. In doing so, churches have neglected the revival and renewal of God's people.

We pray that *Fresh Encounter* will be a tool God will use to bring your church genuine revival. Revival, however, is going to be a recurring need for God's people. We will always be bent toward departing from God and allowing our love relationship with Him to grow cold. Begin now to plan for regular times of revival and renewal. When God brings revival, don't allow the flames to die out again. Guide God's people to return to the Lord regularly. The section "Continuing Renewal" on LM page 50 gives help planning and conducting regular times for renewing the love relationship with God. May this revival/awakening that is coming last generations, or at least until the Lord returns!

14. Prepare for Spiritual Awakening

Once God's people experience genuine revival, we can anticipate a mass spiritual awakening to sweep new converts into our churches. Your church needs to begin preparing for spiritual awakening.

THE INDONESIAN REVIVAL • Avery Willis, author of *MasterLife*, was a missionary in Indonesia during the 1960s. During that time, the Indonesian Revival took place and two million people came to Christ in that Moslem and communistic nation. Following the revival/awakening, Avery studied the revival, looking for the influences God used to bring about such a mass turning to Christ. There were many positive influences, but one of his conclusions was that the churches were not ready.

The churches did not have a strong leadership base. Christians were not discipled sufficiently to help these new Christians grow into mature disciples. Avery concluded that they might have seen twice as many people respond to Christ if the churches had been ready.

In 1978, Avery was asked to return to the United States to help prepare discipleship materials. At first he had no interest in returning because he sensed God was going to judge America for its sins. Avery didn't want to be here when it happened. As he prayed, he sensed that God wanted him to return for a purpose. He sensed God was preparing to bring revival and awakening, but the churches were not ready. He did return with a deep burden to help churches lay a solid foundation of mature disciples so they would be ready for the awakening to come.

God has been working in similar ways through many other leaders and in many denominations preparing us for an outpouring of His Spirit in revival. Our churches need to be prepared.

GET READY • Here are some suggestions you may want to consider as you prepare your people for spiritual awakening.

• *Provide extensive discipleship training at all levels of spiritual growth for your members.* Remember that the task of the Great Commission is not complete until you have taught them to obey all that Christ has commanded (see Matt. 28:19-20).

• *Develop leaders who will be able to teach others.* The task will be too big for a pastor and church staff. Every member of the body needs to be equipped for the ministry of building up the body (see Eph. 4:11-13).

• *Pray that the Lord of the harvest will call forth laborers into the harvest* (see Matt. 9:37-38). Now is the time to pray for leaders and then prepare them for service. If you wait until the awakening comes, you will be behind schedule.

• *Prepare witnesses and commitment counselors.* People who are drawn to Christ in awakening will come asking the question, "What must I do to be saved?" People need to be trained to help them. They, however, should not be trained just to go through a prescribed plan or to lead a certain prayer. These witnesses and commitment counselors need to be spiritual physicians who can guide people to repent of their sins, place their faith and trust in Christ, and surrender to His absolute lordship in their lives.

• *Train new Christian encouragers who will be able to help new believers begin to grow and mature as disciples of Jesus Christ.* The new Christian often experiences pressures and crises that result from conflicts between old and new patterns of living. Christian encouragers can guide new Christians to understand and deal with these conflicts as they help the new Christian develop regular patterns of quiet time, prayer, Bible study, and Scripture memory. The *Survival Kit for New Christians* is an example of a tool to help new Christians grow in their relationship with God.

• *Prepare for an avalanche of ministry needs.* Our world is filled with brokenness. Families are broken and hurting. Often in awakening, the poor and needy are the ones most responsive to the gospel. People who have all kinds of significant needs will be brought into the Kingdom and into your church. You will need to help them understand that the gospel includes more than going to heaven when they die. They need to experience the healing power of Christ at work reconciling relationships, restoring families, healing the pains of the past, and setting them free from bondage to vices of all kinds.

Consider using LIFE Support materials from LifeWay Press to provide Christ-centered support groups for meeting such needs.

Many will have tangible needs for food, clothing, jobs, health care, and housing. The model in the New Testament church is an example for your church. The members gave sacrificially to provide for the needs of others so that "there were no needy persons among them" (Acts 4:34).

- *Prepare your people to make major adjustments.* You are Kingdom people. Anytime God invites you to become involved with Him, you will have to make major adjustments in your life and church. You don't need to be fearful, just obedient and expectant. Using God's Word, prepare your church to accept any cost or adjustment involved in seeing the Kingdom come into the lives of the people in your community. Your church can become a world mission strategy center.
- *Prepare to give God all the glory.* A sure way to shut down revival and spiritual awakening is to claim God's glory for yourself or your church. Recognize that you cannot do what God does in revival and spiritual awakening. When God does it, magnify God in the eyes of His people. Declare His glory among the people. Do not claim any credit for yourself. A careful use of music will help. The songbook, *Return to Me,* can greatly assist you.
- *Prepare yourself and God's people to let Him be in control.* Another way to shut down what God is doing is to try to organize or control it. As a spiritual leader, when revival starts, you will be tempted to control or manage what is taking place. Let the Holy Spirit guide you moment by moment. Adjust your plans and agenda to what God is doing. Work on His timetable, not your own. When God's Spirit is poured out on your people or community, forget your agenda and adjust to what God is doing. If you don't know what to do next, ask for the counsel of other leaders in your church or from the body. God will speak to His body to guide it correctly; you can depend on Him.

15. Introduce *God's Pattern for Revival and Spiritual Awakening*

Once you have prepared for *Fresh Encounter* and you sense God's directions to begin, introduce the church to *God's Pattern for Revival and Spiritual Awakening*. If possible use *Fresh Encounter Introductory Video* and the suggestions for the Introductory Session on LM page 64. Your goal in this introduction is to encourage people to commit to participate actively in the study of *God's Pattern for Revival and Spiritual Awakening*. Because the whole church needs to return to the Lord together, consider how and when a maximum number of people can be introduced to the study. You may want to preach a message God gives you on God's pattern for revival and spiritual awakening during a service before or after you use the video message in preparation for the small-group study.

16. Provide Copies of the Worksheets

Help the small-group leaders by reproducing the needed number of copies of the worksheets used in the study of *God's Pattern for Revival and Spiritual Awakening*. Make these worksheets available to leaders at a central location at the church or distribute them to the leaders before the study. Leaders should encourage the people to use them as a spiritual journey notebook. Again, this is not just a course of study; it is a fresh encounter with God. Have members keep records of what God says and does with them as individuals and church members so they can faithfully respond to Him.

Needed: Spiritual Leaders

As a spiritual leader of God's people, you have a wonderful privilege of being a fellow worker with God in His Kingdom. You also have an awesome responsibility and accountability to God for those He has entrusted to your leadership. Throughout the Scriptures, when God's people departed from Him, God sought out spiritual leaders to guide His people back to a right relationship with Himself. The future of God's people often was dependent on the response of the leadership.

STANDING IN THE GAP

A pattern we see in Scripture is described in Ezekiel 22:30-31. When the people had forsaken God, God said:

> [30]"I looked for a man among them who would build up the wall and stand before me in the gap on behalf of the land so I would not have to destroy it, but I found none. [31]So I will pour out my wrath on them and consume them with my fiery anger, bringing down on their own heads all they have done, declares the Sovereign Lord."

In this case God did not find a spiritual leader willing to stand in the gap *before God* in behalf of the land. So God brought destruction on the land with the fall of Jerusalem to the Babylonians in 587 B.C.

In other cases a spiritual leader responded and the people were spared. For instance, after Israel was miraculously delivered from Egypt, Moses went up on the mountain to receive the law. While he was gone, Aaron and the people rebelled against the Lord and built a golden calf to worship. God said to Moses, "Leave me alone so that my anger may burn against them and that I may destroy them. Then I will make you into a great nation" (Ex. 32:10).

Moses could have been selfish and agreed with God. Then he would have become the father of the nation instead of Abraham. But Moses demonstrated the character of a true spiritual leader when he unselfishly prayed for Israel.

> [11]"O Lord," he said, "why should your anger burn against your people, whom you brought out of Egypt with great power and a mighty hand? . . . [12]Turn from your fierce anger; relent and do not bring disaster on your people."
> –Exodus 32:11-12

God heard Moses' plea on behalf of the people, and "The Lord relented and did not bring on his people the disaster he had threatened" (Ex. 32:14). After the spies brought back a majority report against entering the promised land, the people again rebelled against the Lord. God determined to destroy the people, and Moses prayed for God to spare the people (see Num. 14). A spiritual leader must be prepared to stand unselfishly in the gap before the Lord in behalf of the people—even if the people are sinful and rebellious.

When the people of God are sin-sick, the spiritual character of a leader is put to the test. God never gave Moses permission to leave the people when they were so rebellious. People needed spiritual leadership at those times more than at any other, and great experiences await the leader(s) who will stay with God's people until God completes His work in them and through them.

SPIRITUAL LEADERSHIP IN TIMES OF CRISIS

Many spiritual leaders have looked to the world and popular books on leadership and management to find out what kind of leader they ought to be. The world cannot give you the kind of counsel you need to be a spiritual leader. You need to allow God to mold and shape you into the instrument He can use to care for His people in times of spiritual crisis. God always will be at work shaping your character for any assignment He intends to give you. After God punished Israel by sending them into exile, He said:

> [11]"I know the plans I have for you," declares the Lord, "plans to prosper you and not to harm you, plans to give you hope and a future. [12]Then you will call upon me and come and pray to me, and I will listen to you. [13]You will seek me and find me when you seek me with all your heart."
> –Jeremiah 29:11-13

The crises we face in our churches, our nation, and the world today will require God-prepared, Christ-centered, Holy Spirit-empowered people of prayer. Spiritual leaders must seek God with all their hearts.

These are unique times when God is working mightily worldwide. God is breaking down barriers to the spread of the gospel—political barriers, language barriers, and even technological barriers. We are witnessing the beginnings of one of the greatest moves of God in bringing a lost world to Himself. Casual leadership will not be sufficient. Human-centered leadership will fail. Only God has the counsel for the kind of leader He needs for these important days. Are you willing to let God make you into the kind of leader He needs in times of crisis? What kind of leader does God need? Kingdom leaders!

Jesus Commissioned Twelve Leaders

In Matthew 10 Jesus gave instructions to His twelve disciples to prepare them for the mission on which He was about to send them. This was an inauguration time for the leaders to whom God was going to entrust the future of His Kingdom's work. He gave them guidelines on the cost of spiritual leadership for those critical days. These instructions are just as powerful and relevant today as they were 2,000 years ago. We have identified 14 qualities of the spiritual leaders God is calling out for His redemptive mission in our day.

Qualities of Spiritual Leadership
Matthew 9:35–10:42

1. A sense of urgency (Matt. 9:35-37)
2. A genuine and intense prayer life (Matt. 9:38)
3. An unconditional relationship to Jesus as Lord (Matt. 10:1)
4. An awareness of accountability to God (Matt. 10:1,8)
5. A clear demonstration of spiritual authority (Matt. 10:1,8)
6. Absolute faith, trust, and confidence in God (Matt. 10:9-10)
7. A God-given sense of direction (Matt. 10:5-7,11-16)
8. A clear commitment to the cost involved (Matt. 10:17-23)
9. Absolutely God-oriented (Matt. 10:26-31)
10. A servant life patterned after the Lord Jesus (Matt. 10:24-25)
11. An open witness to Jesus as Lord (Matt. 10:32-33)
12. A willingness to risk for the Kingdom (Matt. 10:34-36)
13. A wholehearted love for God and His Son Jesus (Matt. 10:37-39)
14. A life of unmistakable identity with Jesus Christ (Matt. 10:40-42)

Let's consider each of these in detail.

1. **A Sense of Urgency.** The context for Matthew 10 is found in chapter 9:35-37.

> ³⁵Jesus went through all the towns and villages, teaching in their synagogues, preaching the good news of the kingdom and healing every disease and sickness. ³⁶When he saw the crowds, he had compassion on them, because they were harassed and helpless, like sheep without a shepherd. ³⁷Then he said to his disciples, "The harvest is plentiful but the workers are few."
> –Matthew 9:35-37

Jesus expressed a sense of urgency over the condition of God's people. Spiritual leaders of today must have a God-like sense of urgency. The leader who walks with our Lord will catch the sense of urgency. Jesus was burdened and had compassion for God's people "because they were harassed and helpless, like sheep without a shepherd." This was the desperate condition to which Jesus sent the twelve on mission.

2. **A Genuine and Intense Prayer Life.** When faced with such a severe need for laborers, Jesus told his disciples to pray:

> "Ask the Lord of the harvest, therefore, to send out workers into his harvest field."
> –Matthew 9:38

In times of crisis, a spiritual leader must be a person of genuine, intense, God-called prayer. He must be an intercessor who knows what it means to labor before God in prayer for the people. Even though you may not know what to pray, the Holy Spirit will guide your praying according to the will of God as He intercedes for us (see Rom. 8:26-27). Prayer must become the priority of a leader's work strategy. A leader must also know how to pray for laborers.

A small church in Alaska was studying *Experiencing God: Knowing and Doing the Will of God*. The pastor became convicted that they had forced and manipulated people to take positions of leadership to which God had not called them. He knew the church could not function as a healthy body of Christ unless it was arranged the way Christ the Head wanted it. One Sunday the pastor preached on the need for God-called leaders in the church. For his invitation, he asked all leaders in the 45-member church to pray during the week about their positions of leadership. He asked all leaders who did not sense God had called them to their leadership positions to turn in their resignations the following week. Then the church would pray that God would call forth the laborers He wanted in place.

The next Sunday every leader in the church resigned except two Sunday School teachers. With clear guidelines in Scripture, they began to pray with confidence that God would call forth laborers.

Within two weeks every position in the church was filled by people who sensed God wanted them to serve there.

This kind of bold action required great faith and confidence in the One [Jesus] who said: "Ask the Lord of the harvest, therefore, to send out workers into his harvest field" (Matt. 9:38). Spiritual leaders today must be people who have prayer as a primary work strategy. They must trust in a God who answers prayer. "The one who calls you is faithful and he will do it" (1 Thess. 5:24).

3. **An Unconditional Relationship to Jesus as Lord.** God is faithful to accomplish His work through those He calls. Spiritual leaders must be in an intimate love relationship with Jesus as the sovereign Lord of their lives.

4. **An Awareness of Accountability to God.** As a God-called leader, your number one accountability is to the God who called you. Spiritual leaders must not be swayed by every opinion or pressure group that comes along.

Too many leaders today listen to the opinions of the followers before they are willing to take a stand. That kind of leadership will never do in times of crisis. Like Paul, you must see yourself as a bond slave to Jesus Christ with a high level of accountability to Him.

5. **A Clear Demonstration of Spiritual Authority.** In Matthew 10, Jesus commissioned the spiritual leaders and sent them out.

> ¹He called his twelve disciples to him and gave them authority to drive out evil spirits and to heal every disease and sickness. . . .
> ⁸"Heal the sick, raise the dead, cleanse those who have leprosy, drive out demons. Freely you have received, freely give."
> –Matthew 10:1,8

Spiritual authority comes from Christ, who has the full measure of God within Him. He has taken up residence within a believer to work through him (see Col. 2:9-10). Christ is the One with power and authority who will be at work through spiritual leaders. The term "spiritual authority" has been abused in our day. Do not misunderstand. A spiritual leader will walk in humility. He does not work in his own power or authority nor in the authority that comes with a position. A spiritual leader goes forth in the power and authority that has been given to him by Christ, who is at work through the leader.

As a spiritual leader, you have an incredible dimension of the Father's presence to undergird and strengthen you in everything you do. No crisis will get out of the control of the Heavenly Father. You will be able to stand in the middle of any crisis understanding that God's power and authority will flow through you. You will not have to proclaim your spiritual authority. That power and authority will be evident to all those around you.

6. **An Absolute Faith, Trust, and Confidence in God.**

> ⁹"Do not take along any gold or silver or copper in your belts; ¹⁰take no bag for the journey, or extra tunic, or sandals or a staff; for the worker is worth his keep."
> –Matthew 10:9-10

Jesus explained to the disciples that they had a different set of resources than they had known previously. They would not have to worry about their provisions.

A spiritual leader must have an incredible faith, trust, and confidence in God and in His provision. The God who sends you is also the God who will provide for you. The life-style of a spiritual leader will show confidence like Paul's: "God is able to make all grace abound to you, so that in all things at all times, having all that you need, you will abound in every good work" (2 Cor. 9:8).

You dare not go into the crises of your world without confidence in the God you serve. A God-called leader need never be tentative, hopeless, or despairing in the middle of crisis.

7. **A God-given Sense of Direction.**

> ⁵These twelve Jesus sent out with the following instructions: "Do not go among the Gentiles or enter any town of the Samaritans. ⁶Go rather to the lost sheep of Israel. ⁷As you go, preach this message: 'The kingdom of heaven is near. . . .'
> ¹¹Whatever town or village you enter, search for some worthy person there and stay at his house until you leave. ¹²As you enter the home, give it your greeting. ¹³If the home is deserving, let your peace rest on it; if it is not, let your peace return to you. ¹⁴If anyone will not welcome you or listen to your words, shake the dust off your feet when you leave that home or town. ¹⁵I tell you the truth, it will be more bearable for Sodom and Gomorrah on the day of judgment than for that town. ¹⁶I am sending you out like

sheep among wolves. Therefore be as shrewd as snakes and as innocent as doves."
–Matthew 10:5-7,11-16

When God sends out leaders, He directs them in His ways. God sends them on His terms. God also makes them aware of the awesome consequences of their actions and the actions of those to whom they are sent. A spiritual leader is under no misconception of what is involved in his mission with Christ. Jesus warned the disciples that they would face great distress as they went on mission for Him.

As you follow God's directions, you need to have a sense that God has sent you; that He knows where you will be going; that He knows what you will experience; and that He will be present to guide, direct, and enable you to complete your mission.

8. A Clear Commitment to the Cost Involved.

[17]"Be on your guard against men; they will hand you over to the local councils and flog you in their synagogues. [18]On my account you will be brought before governors and kings as witnesses to them and to the Gentiles. [19]But when they arrest you, do not worry about what to say or how to say it. At that time you will be given what to say, [20]for it will not be you speaking, but the Spirit of your Father speaking through you.

[21]Brother will betray brother to death, and a father his child; children will rebel against their parents and have them put to death. [22]All men will hate you because of me, but he who stands firm to the end will be saved. [23]When you are persecuted in one place, flee to another. I tell you the truth, you will not finish going through the cities of Israel before the Son of Man comes."
–Matthew 10:17-23

Jesus explained the cost of following Him. Jesus knew the times that were coming. He was orienting these leaders to be prepared for the things to come. Yet, the disciples did not need to worry about what to do. He reminded them the Holy Spirit would be present through those difficult circumstances.

Be aware of the great cost of being a spiritual leader. You may not win popularity contests. You must not try to please people, but deliver God's message. Do not back away from obedience just because the cost is high. For example, there will be times during *Fresh Encounter* when you will not know what to say or do. Trust the Holy Spirit to guide you. The Holy Spirit is provided by God to give you all the resources you need when you need them—even in the face of severe opposition.

9. Absolutely God-oriented.

[26]"So do not be afraid of them. There is nothing concealed that will not be disclosed, or hidden that will not be made known. [27]What I tell you in the dark, speak in the daylight; what is whispered in your ear, proclaim from the roofs. [28]Do not be afraid of those who kill the body but cannot kill the soul. Rather, be afraid of the One who can destroy both soul and body in hell. [29]Are not two sparrows sold for a penny? Yet not one of them will fall to the ground apart from the will of your Father. [30]And even the very hairs of your head are all numbered. [31]So don't be afraid; you are worth more than many sparrows."
–Matthew 10:26-31

Jesus wanted these leaders to be God-oriented. They did not need to be afraid of others; they were of great value to God. God knew about the most intimate parts of their lives. God would vindicate the ones He had chosen.

God will be intimate with you as His leader. Nothing will escape His knowledge. The God who controls all history will take care of you. You will never need to be afraid of people or their opinions. They can only kill your body. The One you are to fear is God. You need a healthy fear of Him.

10. A Servant Life Patterned after the Lord Jesus.

[24]"A student is not above his teacher, nor a servant above his master. [25]It is enough for the student to be like his teacher, and the servant like his master. If the head of the house has been called Beelzebub, how much more the members of his household!
[26]So do not be afraid of them."
–Matthew 10:24-26

Jesus told His disciples to pattern their lives after Him. He was their Master. They were servants to Him. A spiritual leader will function in the ways of the Kingdom.

You must pattern your life after Jesus and His Kingdom. Jesus is your absolute Master. You are His servant. Your identity should not be with the world but with your Master. Do not develop your leadership style and qualities from the world but from the Kingdom of God. Do not try to function in the world's ways. The Kingdom's guidelines and ways are different. It will be enough to be like your Master. To pattern your life after Him, however, you must thoroughly study His life under the instruction of the Holy Spirit.

A spiritual leader will be one who shares in the ridicule and sufferings of His Lord. You do not have the option to choose the things about Jesus that you are willing to follow. To be His spiritual leader in a time of crisis you must be ready to share in His cross like Paul who said, "I want to know Christ . . . and the fellowship of sharing in his sufferings, becoming like him in his death" (Phil. 3:10). Would you be willing to identify with the sufferings of Christ? Pray through Isaiah 53 before you answer that question.

This is the kind of requirement God had for spiritual leaders when Jesus came to bring redemption to the world. God did not spare Jesus. Do you suppose that the requirements would be any less when the Lord is preparing to return and bring history to a close? We may be approaching the time in history when a special dimension of spiritual leadership will be required.

11. An Open Witness to Jesus as Lord.

> ³²"Whoever acknowledges me before men, I will also acknowledge him before my Father in heaven. ³³But whoever disowns me before men, I will disown him before my Father in heaven."
> –Matthew 10:32-33

A spiritual leader will have an open witness to Jesus as Lord, among God's people and in a world filled with people who do not believe. This witness does not mean just saying words in favor of Jesus. A spiritual leader must have an authentic life in Christ. He or she must live so that Christ openly displays Himself before a watching world. Paul had such a life-style.

> ²I resolved to know nothing while I was with you except Jesus Christ and him crucified. . . . ⁴My message and my preaching were not with wise and persuasive words, but with a demonstration of the Spirit's power, ⁵so that your faith might not rest on men's wisdom, but on God's power.
> –1 Corinthians 2:2,4-5

Could you describe your life and ministry as a demonstration of the Spirit's power? Or are you depending more on yourself, your wisdom, and your gifts and persuasive words? You must come to the place where the Christ who dwells in you is indeed your life. When your life on the outside reflects Christ on the inside, your open witness to Christ is true. God uses that kind of witness to draw His people to Himself, and men and women to His Son for redemption.

12. A Willingness to Risk for the Kingdom.

> ³⁴"Do not suppose that I have come to bring peace to the earth. I did not come to bring peace, but a sword. ³⁵For I have come to turn
> 'a man against his father,
>   a daughter against her mother,
> a daughter-in-law against her mother-in-law—
> ³⁶a man's enemies will be the members
>   of his own household.' "
> –Matthew 10:34-36

A spiritual leader will be a person willing to risk for the Kingdom. He will be unafraid of others' opinions. He will be ready for spiritual warfare.

Not everyone will be with you when you are following God. Your enemies may even be people in your own household. You must be ready in a time of crisis for a quality of spiritual warfare that may test every intimate relationship you have. Yet, you must be willing to risk with your eyes wide open to the possible conflict.

Jesus said, "For judgment I have come into this world" (John 9:39). Notice that when Jesus sends you out with a message like that, He does not bring peace but a sword. You will face spiritual warfare. Will you be willing to risk all, including your life, to deliver that message obediently, especially to God's people?

13. A Wholehearted Love for God and His Son Jesus.

> ³⁷"Anyone who loves his father or mother more than me is not worthy of me; anyone who loves his son or daughter more than me is not worthy of me; ³⁸and anyone who does not take his cross and follow me is not worthy of me. ³⁹Whoever finds his life will lose it, and whoever loses his life for my sake will find it."
> –Matthew 10:37-39

Jesus knew the world into which these leaders were going. He deliberately called them into the kind of a life-style that would require a cross. He knew that the crosses for many of these leaders would be their lives. Yet, Jesus knew that the future of the Kingdom of God was going to rest on the quality of the love relationship these men had with Him.

Jesus hid nothing from these leaders. The call would be real. The power would be real. The authority would be real. His presence would be real. The enemy would be real. The demands would be real. The cross would be real.

In a time of crisis, a spiritual leader will have a wholehearted love for God and His Son that exceeds all other affections. Your love relationship is to be uncontested by any other relationship in your life, including your love for your own life. Wholehearted love is the only love relationship that is worthy of Christ. The love of Christ will compel you to serve Him. But that love relationship will require a cross. The will of God is the cross. Self-will must be crucified to follow Him. Be careful that you do not turn aside from the will of God when the cross becomes real.

14. A Life of Unmistakable Identity with Jesus Christ.

> [40] "He who receives you receives me, and he who receives me receives the one who sent me. [41] Anyone who receives a prophet because he is a prophet will receive a prophet's reward, and anyone who receives a righteous man because he is a righteous man will receive a righteous man's reward. [42] And if anyone gives even a cup of cold water to one of these little ones because he is my disciple, I tell you the truth, he will certainly not lose his reward."
> –Matthew 10:40-42

Jesus called the disciples to a clear and unmistakable identity with Him. They would be in union with Jesus, taking on the nature, pattern, and lifestyle of their living Lord. They knew, however, that this would bring them into conflict with the attitudes and religious practices of their day. They also knew that Jesus stood ready to reward the faithful servant. A day of accountability would come.

A spiritual leader will do everything with a clear anticipation of accountability before his Lord. The consuming passion of your heart should be to hear on that day, "Well done, good and faithful servant" (Matt. 25:21).

Summary

We need spiritual leaders as described above today in the crisis in which we find ourselves. God's pattern for spiritual leadership is clear; it is not hidden. The cost factors are not hidden. The resources of God are not hidden. The love relationship is not hidden. From the call, to the empowering, to the going out, to what you will encounter, to the identification with the pattern of Jesus, to the open witness, to the fact that the work will not be easy, God reveals His requirements for spiritual leadership in times of crisis. With all this in mind, you can know you have a message that means life and death to those who hear. The church waits for this kind of leader, and the world waits for the messenger who comes with an authentic call and message demonstrating the power and authority of the One who sent him. The message is this: "Repent, for the kingdom of heaven is near" (Matt. 4:17).

A spiritual leader is . .
. . a person of intensity with a sense of urgency.
. . a person of integrity before God and men.
. . a person of involvement in the mission of Christ.
. . a person of intercession who is known in the courts of God.
. . a person of interdependence with the people of God.
. . a person of influence with God.

Consider this prayer for your life as a leader.

> Lord, whatever it costs me, I release my life and our church to you. Guide me to be your spiritual leader during these times of crisis. Do with me what you will. Amen.

N O T E S

A Plumb Line for Shepherds

Pastors, church staff members, and in a sense Sunday School teachers, deacons, elders, discipleship leaders, and other leaders in a church have a role in being shepherds to the people they serve. The following passages describe the kind of shepherd God desires and the kind He despises. Reading about the reasons God liked or did not like spiritual leaders of the past should help you evaluate how He views your work as a spiritual leader.

◆ Take time to pray before beginning to read and respond to the Scriptures and statements that follow. Pray that God will help you see how you measure up to His plumb line for shepherds of His people.

◆ Read the following Scriptures related to shepherds. Use the statements after each passage to evaluate your role as a shepherd. Evaluate each statement as follows:

↑ = I measure up to God's plumb line.
↓ = I need God's help with this plumb line.

If God surfaces areas where you have departed from His plumb line, repent and ask God to give you a heart like His for His people. Ask God to enable you to be a shepherd who is pleasing to Him.

NUMBERS 27:16-17 ◆ ¹⁶"May the Lord, the God of the spirits of all mankind, appoint a man over this community ¹⁷to go out and come in before them, one who will lead them out and bring them in, so the Lord's people will not be like sheep without a shepherd."

_____ I am guiding God's people to be what God wants them to be.

1 SAMUEL 3:19,21 ◆ ¹⁹The Lord was with Samuel as he grew up, and he let none of his words fall to the ground. . . . ²¹The Lord continued to appear at Shiloh, and there he revealed himself to Samuel through his word.

_____ I am faithful like Samuel—I remember and apply any of the words God speaks to me.
_____ God clearly speaks to me through His Word.

PSALM 23:1-6 ◆
¹The Lord is my shepherd, I shall not be in want.
    ²He makes me lie down in green pastures,
he leads me beside quiet waters,
    ³he restores my soul.
He guides me in paths of righteousness
    for his name's sake.
⁴Even though I walk
    through the valley of the shadow of death,
I will fear no evil,
    for you are with me;
your rod and your staff,
    they comfort me.
⁵You prepare a table before me
    in the presence of my enemies.
You anoint my head with oil;
    my cup overflows.
⁶Surely goodness and love will follow me
    all the days of my life,
and I will dwell in the house of the Lord
    forever.

_____ I guide people to Christ and His Word in such a way that their hunger is satisfied with the Bread of life and their thirst with the living Water.
_____ I guide them in paths of righteousness through the model of my own life.
_____ I help people find comfort in God even in the shadow of death.
_____ I guide them into God's presence in such a way that He overflows their spiritual cups.

PSALM 78:70-72 ◆
⁷⁰He chose David his servant
    and took him from the sheep pens;
⁷¹from tending the sheep he brought him
    to be the shepherd of his people Jacob,
    of Israel his inheritance.
⁷²And David shepherded them with integrity of heart;
    with skillful hands he led them.

_____ I shepherd God's people with integrity of heart and skillful hands.

ISAIAH 40:11 •
He tends his flock like a shepherd:
  He gathers the lambs in his arms
and carries them close to his heart;
  he gently leads those that have young.

_____ I love God's people and gently lead them. I do not have hard feelings toward them or treat them harshly.

ISAIAH 56:10-11 •
¹⁰Israel's watchmen are blind,
  they all lack knowledge;
they are all mute dogs,
  they cannot bark;
they lie around and dream,
  they love to sleep.
¹¹They are dogs with mighty appetites;
  they never have enough.
They are shepherds who lack
    understanding;
  they all turn to their own way,
  each seeks his own gain.

_____ I am a faithful watchman, alerting God's people of any impending danger.
_____ I have a knowledge of God's ways and requirements.
_____ I do not have a strong appetite for personal gain that is never satisfied.
_____ I have not turned to my own way.

JEREMIAH 2:8 •
The priests did not ask,
  'Where is the Lord?'
Those who deal with the law did not
    know me;
  the leaders rebelled against me.
The prophets prophesied by Baal,
  following worthless idols.

_____ I regularly ask, "Where is the Lord?" I seek His presence and directions.
_____ I know God by experience in an intimate and personal way.
_____ I have not rebelled against God's leadership or lordship over me or over His people.
_____ I have not followed after worthless idols, especially idols of the heart.

JEREMIAH 3:14 • "Return, faithless people," declares the Lord, "for I am your husband. I will choose you—one from a town and two from a clan—and bring you to Zion."

_____ I allow God to make me a shepherd after His own heart. I lead with knowledge and understanding of God, His purposes, and His ways.

JEREMIAH 10:21 •
The shepherds are senseless
  and do not inquire of the Lord;
so they do not prosper
  and all their flock is scattered.

_____ Prayer is my primary planning strategy; I ask God for every direction and wait until He shows me.
_____ My flock is prospering. The people are not being scattered.

JEREMIAH 12:10-11 •
¹⁰Many shepherds will ruin my vineyard
  and trample down my field;
they will turn my pleasant field
  into a desolate wasteland.
¹¹It will be made a wasteland,
  parched and desolate before me;
the whole land will be laid waste
  because there is no one who cares.

_____ I have done more to build up God's people than to tear them down. They are stronger, not weaker, because of my leadership. I care for them.

JEREMIAH 23:1-4 • ¹"Woe to the shepherds who are destroying and scattering the sheep of my pasture!" declares the Lord. ²Therefore this is what the Lord, the God of Israel, says to the shepherds who tend my people: "Because you have scattered my flock and driven them away and have not bestowed care on them, I will bestow punishment on you for the evil you have done," declares the Lord. ³"I myself will gather the remnant of my flock out of all the countries where I have driven them and will bring them back to their pasture, where they will be fruitful and increase in number. ⁴I will place shepherds over them who will tend them, and they will no longer be afraid or terrified, nor will any be missing," declares the Lord.

_____ I am strengthening rather than destroying the sheep.
_____ I am gathering rather than scattering the sheep.
_____ I am bestowing care on the sheep rather than driving them away.

_____ None of my sheep are afraid, terrified, or missing.

_____ I am taking care of the sheep God has already given me. (Healthy and contented sheep are fruitful and multiply.)

JEREMIAH 25:34-36 •

³⁴Weep and wail, you shepherds;
>   roll in the dust, you leaders of the flock.
> For your time to be slaughtered has come;
>   you will fall and be shattered like fine pottery.
> ³⁵The shepherds will have nowhere to flee,
>   the leaders of the flock no place to escape.
> ³⁶Hear the cry of the shepherds,
>   the wailing of the leaders of the flock,
>   for the Lord is destroying their pasture.

_____ I am aware of my accountability to God for the sheep entrusted to me.

_____ I fear God.

JEREMIAH 50:6-7 •

⁶"My people have been lost sheep;
>   their shepherds have led them astray
>   and caused them to roam on the mountains.
> They wandered over mountain and hill
>   and forgot their own resting place.
> ⁷Whoever found them devoured them;
>   their enemies said, 'We are not guilty,
>   for they sinned against the Lord, their true pasture,
>   the Lord, the hope of their fathers.' "

_____ I have not led the people astray. I have not guided them to do things that are not part of God's purposes for His people. I have not led them to devote their time to activities that distract from God's work.

_____ The people have not forgotten their mission.

_____ The people have not forgotten their resting place. They have not strayed from an intimate and personal relationship with God.

_____ My sheep are not wandering from church to church with no firm resting place.

_____ My sheep are not being devoured by enemies like crime, abuse, bankruptcy, or sin's consequences.

EZEKIEL 34:2-6 •

²"Son of man, prophesy against the shepherds of Israel; prophesy and say to them: 'This is what the Sovereign Lord says: Woe to the shepherds of Israel who only take care of themselves! Should not shepherds take care of the flock? ³You eat the curds, clothe yourselves with the wool and slaughter the choice animals, but you do not take care of the flock. ⁴You have not strengthened the weak or healed the sick or bound up the injured. You have not brought back the strays or searched for the lost. You have ruled them harshly and brutally. ⁵So they were scattered because there was no shepherd, and when they were scattered they became food for all the wild animals. ⁶My sheep wandered over all the mountains and on every high hill. They were scattered over the whole earth, and no one searched or looked for them."

_____ I am not more concerned about taking care of myself than about taking care of God's sheep.

_____ I have strengthened the weak, healed the sick, and bound up the injured.

_____ I have brought back the strays or searched for the lost. I have not said, "When they get right with the Lord, they will come back."

_____ I have not ruled them harshly or brutally.

_____ They are not being devoured by wild animals like divorce, adultery, greed, materialism, envy, and strife.

EZEKIEL 34:7-10 •

⁷" 'Therefore, you shepherds, hear the word of the Lord: ⁸As surely as I live, declares the Sovereign Lord, because my flock lacks a shepherd and so has been plundered and has become food for all the wild animals, and because my shepherds did not search for my flock but cared for themselves rather than for my flock, ⁹therefore, O shepherds, hear the word of the Lord: ¹⁰This is what the Sovereign Lord says: I am against the shepherds and will hold them accountable for my flock. I will remove them from tending the flock so that the shepherds can no longer feed themselves. I will rescue my flock from their mouths, and it will no longer be food for them.' "

_____ I know God holds me accountable for the condition of His sheep.

_____ I know God has never been the source of any resistance I have experienced.

_____ I have not experienced attempts to be removed from my leadership role. I realize that such attempts could be God's discipline.

_____ I am not experiencing personal financial problems that could be God's discipline for unfaithfulness.

> EZEKIEL 34:11-16 • ¹¹" 'For this is what the Sovereign Lord says: I myself will search for my sheep and look after them. ¹²As a shepherd looks after his scattered flock when he is with them, so will I look after my sheep. I will rescue them from all the places where they were scattered on a day of clouds and darkness. ¹³I will bring them out from the nations and gather them from the countries, and I will bring them into their own land. I will pasture them on the mountains of Israel, in the ravines and in all the settlements in the land. ¹⁴I will tend them in a good pasture, and the mountain heights of Israel will be their grazing land. There they will lie down in good grazing land, and there they will feed in a rich pasture on the mountains of Israel. ¹⁵I myself will tend my sheep and have them lie down, declares the Sovereign Lord. ¹⁶I will search for the lost and bring back the strays. I will bind up the injured and strengthen the weak, but the sleek and the strong I will destroy. I will shepherd the flock with justice.' "

_____ I am the kind of shepherd God wants for His sheep. I model what a godly shepherd will do for the flock.

> ZECHARIAH 10:2-3 •
> ²The idols speak deceit,
>   diviners see visions that lie;
> they tell dreams that are false,
>   they give comfort in vain.
> Therefore the people wander like sheep
>   oppressed for lack of a shepherd.
> ³"My anger burns against the shepherds,
>   and I will punish the leaders;
> for the Lord Almighty will care
>   for his flock, the house of Judah,
>   and make them like a proud horse in battle."

_____ I have not allowed the people to be deceived by false teaching.

_____ The people have not turned to false gods and come into bondage and oppression for their sins.

> MARK 6:34 • When Jesus landed and saw a large crowd, he had compassion on them, because they were like sheep without a shepherd. So he began teaching them many things.

_____ I have compassion on the scattered sheep.
_____ I am teaching them about the Kingdom and God's ways.

> LUKE 15:4-7 • ⁴"Suppose one of you has a hundred sheep and loses one of them. Does he not leave the ninety-nine in the open country and go after the lost sheep until he finds it? ⁵And when he finds it, he joyfully puts it on his shoulders ⁶and goes home. Then he calls his friends and neighbors together and says, 'Rejoice with me; I have found my lost sheep.' ⁷I tell you that in the same way there will be more rejoicing in heaven over one sinner who repents than over ninety-nine righteous persons who do not need to repent."

_____ I am willing to leave the sheep who are safe to go after the ones who have gone astray—the ones who are inactive.

_____ I have shown concern for the nonresident members in my church who may need to transfer to another flock so they can be cared for.

> JOHN 10:2-5,11-15 • ²"The man who enters by the gate is the shepherd of his sheep. ³The watchman opens the gate for him, and the sheep listen to his voice. He calls his own sheep by name and leads them out. ⁴When he has brought out all his own, he goes on ahead of them, and his sheep follow him because they know his voice. ⁵But they will never follow a stranger; in fact, they will run away from him because they do not recognize a stranger's voice."
> ¹¹"I am the good shepherd. The good shepherd lays down his life for the sheep. ¹²The hired hand is not the shepherd who owns the sheep. So when he sees the wolf coming, he abandons the sheep and runs away. Then the wolf attacks the flock and scatters it. ¹³The man runs away because he is a hired hand and cares nothing for the sheep.
> ¹⁴"I am the good shepherd; I know my sheep and my sheep know me—¹⁵just as the Father knows me and I know the Father—and I lay down my life for the sheep."

_____ I love the sheep enough to willingly give my life in service to them. I do not run away when the going gets tough because I am just a hired hand working for the money.

◆ The following Scriptures are especially directed to the pastors and overseers of the flock.

> JOHN 21:15 • When they had finished eating, Jesus said to Simon Peter, "Simon son of John, do you truly love me more than these?"
>
> "Yes, Lord," he said, "you know that I love you."
>
> Jesus said, "Feed my lambs."

_____ I love Jesus, and I am feeding His lambs.

> ACTS 20:28-30 • 28"Keep watch over yourselves and all the flock of which the Holy Spirit has made you overseers. Be shepherds of the church of God, which he bought with his own blood. 29I know that after I leave, savage wolves will come in among you and will not spare the flock. 30Even from your own number men will arise and distort the truth in order to draw away disciples after them."

_____ I am keeping watch over the flock and protecting them from the wild animals that destroy and the false teachers who lead astray.

> 1 TIMOTHY 3:1-7 • 1Here is a trustworthy saying: If anyone sets his heart on being an overseer, he desires a noble task. 2Now the overseer must be above reproach, the husband of but one wife, temperate, self-controlled, respectable, hospitable, able to teach, 3not given to drunkenness, not violent but gentle, not quarrelsome, not a lover of money. 4He must manage his own family well and see that his children obey him with proper respect. 5(If anyone does not know how to manage his own family, how can he take care of God's church?) 6He must not be a recent convert, or he may become conceited and fall under the same judgment as the devil. 7He must also have a good reputation with outsiders, so that he will not fall into disgrace and into the devil's trap.

_____ I am above reproach both inside and outside the church, in public and in private. I have a good reputation with outsiders.

_____ I am the husband of one wife.

_____ I am temperate, self-controlled, respectable, hospitable, able to teach, and not given to drunkenness.

_____ I am gentle and not violent.

_____ I am able to manage my own family. My children obey and respect me.

_____ I am a mature convert.

> TITUS 1:6-11 • 6An elder must be blameless, the husband of but one wife, a man whose children believe and are not open to the charge of being wild and disobedient. 7Since an overseer is entrusted with God's work, he must be blameless—not overbearing, not quick-tempered, not given to drunkenness, not violent, not pursuing dishonest gain. 8Rather he must be hospitable, one who loves what is good, who is self-controlled, upright, holy and disciplined. 9He must hold firmly to the trustworthy message as it has been taught, so that he can encourage others by sound doctrine and refute those who oppose it.
>
> 10For there are many rebellious people, mere talkers and deceivers, especially those of the circumcision group. 11They must be silenced, because they are ruining whole households by teaching things they ought not to teach—and that for the sake of dishonest gain.

_____ I am blameless.
_____ I am not overbearing.
_____ I am patient.
_____ I am holy and disciplined.
_____ I am able to encourage others with sound doctrine.
_____ I am not rebellious or deceiving.
_____ I do not serve for the sake of dishonest gain.

> 1 PETER 5:1-7 • 1To the elders among you, I appeal as a fellow elder, a witness of Christ's sufferings and one who also will share in the glory to be revealed: 2Be shepherds of God's flock that is under your care, serving as overseers—not because you must, but because you are willing, as God wants you to be; not greedy for money, but eager to serve; 3not lording it over those entrusted to you, but being examples to the flock. 4And when the Chief Shepherd appears, you will receive the crown of glory that will never fade away.
>
> 5Young men, in the same way be submis-

sive to those who are older. All of you, clothe yourselves with humility toward one another, because,

"God opposes the proud but gives grace to the humble."

⁶Humble yourselves, therefore, under God's mighty hand, that he may lift you up in due time. ⁷Cast all your anxiety on him because he cares for you.

_____ I do not serve out of duty, but out of love.

_____ I am not working more for money than the pleasure of service.

_____ I do not lead by my position and authority but by my example.

_____ I am not proud and arrogant, but humble and submissive.

_____ I cast my burdens and anxiety on the Lord because He cares for me.

M Y   R E S P O N S E

Pastor's Preparation Guide

Much has already been said about leader preparation for *Fresh Encounter*. This section provides special suggestions and counsel for pastors.

THE IMPORTANCE OF A SPIRITUAL LEADER
Serving as a leader of God's people is a special privilege and a great responsibility. Though every believer has direct access and accountability to God, a spiritual leader carries significant responsibility for the condition of God's people.

God's people have a tendency to depart from Him. One role of a spiritual leader is to be a spiritual physician. A pastor needs to let God work through him to reveal the spiritual needs and to bring His people to spiritual health.

In the Old Testament, God's response to His people was often determined by the life of the leader. For example:

- When Israel built and worshiped a golden calf, God was prepared to destroy them. Then Moses begged God not to bring this disaster on the people. God punished but did not destroy the people because of His leader, Moses (see Ex. 32).
- During David's reign a three-year famine plagued the land. David sought the Lord's perspective. God said it was because King Saul had broken Israel's covenant with the Gibeonites by trying to annihilate them. Saul's sin brought disaster even after his death. David sought to be reconciled with the Gibeonites. "After that, God answered prayer in behalf of the land" (2 Sam. 21:14).
- David decided to take a census of his fighting men against the counsel of Joab. David recognized his sin and asked God for forgiveness, but God first brought a plague on the land that cost the lives of 70,000 people (see 2 Sam. 24).
- Because of their rebellion against God, Israel fell to the Assyrians. Hezekiah, King of Judah, came humbly to the Lord in prayer on behalf of the people. God sent an angel who destroyed 185,000 Assyrian soldiers, and Jerusalem was spared (see 2 Kings 18–19).
- After Hezekiah, Manasseh became king. He was wicked. The people also had sinned, but Manasseh crossed over God's line of grace. God said, "Manasseh king of Judah has committed these detestable sins. He has done more evil than the Amorites who preceded him and has led Judah into sin with his idols. Therefore . . . I am going to bring such disaster on Jerusalem and Judah that the ears of everyone who hears of it will tingle" (2 Kings 21:10-12).
- After God had determined to bring destruction on Jerusalem and Judah, Josiah led the people back to the Lord (see 2 Chron. 34). Because of Josiah's humility and responsiveness to God, God promised not to bring the disaster during his lifetime. "As long as he lived, they did not fail to follow the Lord, the God of their fathers" (2 Chron. 34:33).

Spiritual leadership carries with it accountability to God. In New Testament times, a problem arose when people sought to be spiritual leaders for reasons other than a call of God. James warned, "Not many of you should presume to be teachers, my brothers, because you know that we who teach will be judged more strictly" (Jas. 3:1). James went on to explain to spiritual leaders how powerful the tongue is. Like the little rudder that can direct a large ship, the tongue of a spiritual leader can influence the direction of a church for right or wrong.

A pastor has a great responsibility for the spiritual welfare of the believers entrusted to him. In a sense, he is given stewardship over them. Paul gave some sober counsel to leaders: "It is required that those who have been given a trust must prove faithful. . . . It is the Lord who judges me. . . . He will bring to light what is hidden in darkness and will expose the motives of men's hearts" (1 Cor. 4:2,4-5).

Jesus said, "From everyone who has been given much, much will be demanded; and from the one who has been entrusted with much, much more will be asked" (Luke 12:48). The role of a spiritual leader calls for a holy life and a pure heart before God. His leadership of God's people may mean the difference in their love relationship to God.

REVIVAL OF GOD'S PEOPLE BEGINS WITH A LEADER
In the Bible, revivals always were led by spiritual leaders. Our prayer for you is that God would do such a work of revival in your heart that your church would follow your leadership to a love relationship with the Lord.

◆ Take your copy of *God's Pattern for Revival and Spiritual Awakening* and read about the "Revival Under Josiah and Hilkiah" (GP pp. 80–81).
◆ Would you be willing to humble yourself, pray, seek God's face, and turn from every wicked way in

your life so that God could bring revival to your church as God promised in 2 Chronicles 7:14? Share your commitment to the Lord in prayer right now.

◆ If time permits, turn to LM page 30 and work through "A Plumb Line for Shepherds." This may be a major project for you. Study this plumb line at a time when you can retreat from interruptions and spend ample time with God. This may be your invitation for personal revival as a spiritual leader. If God brings great conviction during this study, remember that any call by God to repentance brings an invitation to revival. It is a clear demonstration of God's love for you. Let God use this time as a refiner would use fire so you may be a vessel of pure gold—one prepared for His service. Repentance in the Bible is one of God's most positive invitations, because it is accompanied by "for the Kingdom of God is near you" (Luke 10:9).

OTHER SUGGESTIONS FOR PREPARATION

You may want to consider some of the following suggestions to help you prepare for leading your church to a fresh encounter with God.

- If you have not already done so, consider studying *Experiencing God: Knowing and Doing the Will of God*. This course is a tool God is greatly using. It may help you hear God's voice more clearly and better understand ways to guide God's people into intimacy with Him.
- Find a godly pastor or other leader you respect for his or her spiritual maturity. Put your life alongside this leader as a prayer partner and a counselor. Help each other as you lead God's people to encounter Him.
- Work diligently to confront any pride in your life. The hour is late. Time is short. Live with a sense of urgency and humbly stand before God. Keep a clear and clean heart before God.
- Determine at the beginning of this experience that you are more interested in pleasing God than people. If you struggle with that commitment, stay before God until He gives you that desire (see Phil. 2:13).
- Take a personal prayer retreat. Get away from the busy life of home and church to spend time with your Heavenly Father. Focus on your love relationship with God. Let God guide the agenda of your praying (see Rom. 8:26-27).
- Review the qualities of a spiritual leader from Matthew 9–10 (LM p. 24). Ask God to develop those characteristics in you for His glory.
- Like Paul, ask people to pray for you at every opportunity.

DO YOU NEED TO BE SET FREE FROM YOUR PAST?

Statistics indicate that from 60 to 80 percent of today's pastors grew up in a hurting home environment. God often uses the pain of that experience to sensitize a person to the hurts of others. However, unresolved pain from your past can become a spiritual stronghold that hinders effective ministry.

One pastor shared how he grew up with an abusive stepfather. Home was often chaotic. Love and approval were based on conditions that could never quite be met. He seldom heard words of encouragement or praise. Most frequently he heard words of criticism and condemnation.

Years later in his ministry, he reached a point of physical, emotional, and spiritual burnout. He described himself as a highly critical person. He was one who always had to be in control. He was sensitive to any disagreement or constructive criticism and took such statements as a personal attack. He was a perfectionist and a workaholic. No matter how successful he was, he never felt any peace or satisfaction from his work. He felt inferior to others. He was always trying to get people to love him, but he would never allow them to get too close. He was lonely and frustrated. He was constantly berating himself for not being good enough.

He was on the verge of a breakdown when some friends encouraged him to get help. In great humility and brokenness, he shared his life story with a small group of friends who provided spiritual counsel. One of those men helped him realize that he never experienced love from his father or stepfather. He then saw that he had responded to God the same way he had to them. He received his Heavenly Father's unconditional love. They prayed with and for him, and he was set free by God's grace.

Causes of Pain. A variety of problems in your past could be affecting your relationship with God and your ministry with God's people. We have seen individuals and leaders who have been in spiritual bondage because of physical, emotional, or sexual abuse in their childhood. Divorce, death of a parent, abandonment by a parent, or even a long-term serious illness can have a strong influence on a person.

If you grew up in an environment like one of these, you may have a tendency to shrug it off and say, "I'm over that now." If, however, you have problems similar to the pastor described above, or if you have problems with most of your relationships with others, you may still be responding out of a painful past. Your love relationship with God may be affected. You may have difficulty being intimate with God or may have trouble trusting Him.

God's Love. Your Heavenly Father wants to set you free from your past to become all He has planned. Often God will allow a person to "hit the bottom" until he or she finally realizes that there is no hope apart from God. At that point, a person is in a condition to experience some of the fullest dimensions of God's love.

God's Solution. Certainly if you have sinned in your anger, developed a root of bitterness, hurt others, or sinned in any way, you are accountable for your actions. You need God's forgiveness. God promises, "If we confess our sins, he is faithful and just and will forgive us our sins and purify us from all unrighteousness" (1 John 1:9). However, you probably need more than forgiveness; you need to be healed and set free.

Growing up in a hurtful home can leave some tender, open wounds that carry into adulthood. It does not matter whether the problems were due to sin (like alcoholism) or due to unfortunate circumstances (like an invalid parent). You may still be affected by the dynamics of that time. Your pain may be expressed in your need to control everything and everyone around you. It might show up in a critical spirit or workaholism. God wants to heal you and set you free. Here are some steps you may want to take.

1. **"Confess your faults one to another, and pray** one for another, that ye may be healed. The effectual fervent prayer of a righteous man availeth much" (Jas. 5:16, KJV). Sometimes you need the prayers of others to receive God's healing work in your life. God may require the involvement of others so you will not think that you somehow earned His favor. God's love is freely given.

2. **Allow God to demolish this spiritual stronghold.** Recognize that God has given spiritual weapons to demolish strongholds like this one.

> "Though we live in the world, we do not wage war as the world does. The weapons we fight with . . . have divine power to demolish strongholds. We demolish arguments and every pretension that sets itself up against the knowledge of God, and we take captive every thought to make it obedient to Christ" (2 Cor. 10:3-5).

A believer with the power and authority of the indwelling Christ has divine weapons. Watch for a person of faith who will pray for you. Share your need and ask him to pray. The prayer of a righteous person is highly effective in the courts of God. Bring every thought in your life and ministry and make it obedient to Christ.

3. **Put the past behind you.** Paul talked to the Philippians about his past, but he determined to not let his past keep him from experiencing God's fullness. His goal was to know Christ and His power. So Paul said, "Forgetting what is behind and straining toward what is ahead, I press on toward the goal to win the prize for which God has called me heavenward in Christ Jesus" (Phil. 3:13-14).

God created you for eternity. God wants to work in the present to conform you to the image of His Son, Jesus. The focus of your attention needs to be on Christ and eternity. When you focus on your painful past you are facing the wrong direction, and your whole life will seem out of sorts. You need to turn away from your past and the pain or abuse you experienced. You need to turn toward God and eternity. Though you will not forget the past, you can treat it as dead and without influence in your present. Focus your attention on Jesus and allow God to remake you in His likeness.

4. **Receive your Heavenly Father's love and healing.** Often a person who has been abused in some way by a parent—especially a father—has trouble feeling close to God the Father. Though you intellectually may know that God's love is pure, safe, trustworthy, unconditional, and free, you may have trouble experiencing His love that way. You may treat your Heavenly Father like you do (or did) your earthly father. You may crave God's love and acceptance yet keep Him at a distance for fear of getting hurt.

To really know God's love you must experience it. God is standing ready to lavish His love on you. God just needs you to allow Him. In order to experience God's love, you need some uninterrupted time with your Heavenly Father.

Go to a place where you can have an extended period alone with Him. Don't try to word some special prayer. God's love is entirely free. Nothing you can do will prompt God to love you—so don't do anything. Just spend time with your Heavenly Father and open your life freely to receive all the love He wants to bestow. Spending this time may be unusual to you. God will be able to convince you of His love. He will bind up your brokenness. He will heal the hurts of your past. God will spiritually lift you into His lap and wrap His loving arms around you. There, surrounded by God's presence you will begin to experience the life-giving dimensions of the unconditional love of a Heavenly Father.

Healing for the Shepherds. The above suggestions are not a rigid set of steps. They describe a love relationship with an Almighty God. He is the only One who can heal the brokenness or pain you sense. Very likely, God will do His healing work through the prayers of other believers (see Jas. 5:16). This is not something you can do on your own. Trust your loving Father. Ask God to guide you to a fellow believer who can help.

We sense that God wants to heal the shepherds so He can cause His healing love to flow through them to His people. If you are a wounded shepherd, let God set you free from your past and heal the hurt or brokenness of your life. God is "the Father of compassion and the God of all comfort, who comforts us in all our troubles, so that we can comfort those in any trouble with the comfort we ourselves have received from God" (2 Cor. 1:3-4).

◆ Take a journal or a pad of paper and begin making a list of all the blessings and spiritual resources God has given you or made available to you. Read through Ephesians 1–3 and Colossians 1–2 and list every blessing or resource God has provided. Spend a period of time in praise and thanksgiving. Agree with God that He has made available all the resources of heaven to accomplish His spiritual purposes through Christ in you and in His church. A fresh encounter with God is impossible to accomplish by yourself. With God all things are possible!

N O T E S

Biblical Foundations for Revival Services

Old Testament Assemblies

In Old Testament times, God knew His people would depart from their fellowship with Him. Their hearts would lose their love for the Lord. Consequently, God made provision for regular times to be set aside for corporate renewal of fellowship. These times of renewal were called holy convocations or sacred assemblies.

Sacred assemblies were days for God's people to come together for a sacred task. They were prescribed as times to:

- demonstrate obedience to God and His commands and decrees.
- remember God's provisions for His people.
- acknowledge God's ownership of all one's resources (time and material).
- offer sacrifice.
- recognize God in His holiness.
- confess and repent of personal and corporate sin.
- renew fellowship and the covenant with God.

Leviticus 23 and Numbers 28–29 identify seven prescribed days each year that were to be celebrated as sacred assemblies.

1. First day of the Feast of the Passover (15th day of the first month)
2. Seventh day of the Feast of the Passover (21st day of the first month)
3. Feast of Firstfruits (Pentecost—50 days after Passover)
4. Feast of Trumpets (1st day of the seventh month)
5. Day of Atonement (10th day of the seventh month)
6. First day of the Feast of Tabernacles (15th day of the seventh month)
7. Eighth day of the Feast of Tabernacles (22nd day of the seventh month)

In addition to these seven annual events designed to maintain close fellowship with God, the Sabbath Day also was to function as a sacred assembly. When these prescribed days accomplished their intended purpose, God's people stayed in right relationship to Him. When the days became mere ritual or religious tradition, they did not do the intended work of bringing the people back into fellowship with God. God condemned these evil assemblies (see Isa. 1:13). Consequently, God often had to bring a loving discipline in order to call them back to Himself.

In the face of God's remedial judgments, the prophet Joel knew the people needed to return to the Lord quickly. He issued a call to an emergency assembly for the people to hurry back to the Lord. God answered by forgiving and restoring His people; He said, "I will repay you for the years the locusts have eaten" (Joel 2:25). God revives His repentant people.

God's desire, however, is that His people would renew their fellowship with Him on a regular, continuing basis. Several of the Old Testament revivals took place on these scheduled days.

New Testament Assemblies

The term *sacred assembly* does not appear in the New Testament. Because the Jerusalem Christians were primarily of Jewish ancestry, they continued to practice the Jewish customs and laws. More than likely, they continued for years to celebrate the times of the Jewish feasts. Two New Testament events occurred in connection with prescribed Jewish sacred assemblies. Both were occasions of great importance to the early church.

Pentecost. After Jesus ascended to heaven, the Jerusalem Christians spent ten days praying and waiting on the coming of the Holy Spirit. On the Day of Pentecost, these Jewish Christians would have been observing a prescribed sacred assembly. During this assembly, the Holy Spirit came and the church was empowered. Peter preached a message from the book of Joel that describes a call to sacred assembly before God. Three thousand converts came to Christ that first day (see Acts 2).

Peter's Deliverance. When King Herod began to persecute the church and executed James, it so pleased the Jews that he arrested Peter with the intention of executing him also. Because it was the Feast of Unleavened Bread (Passover week), Herod put Peter in prison to try him the day after the Passover celebrations ended. The last day of Passover (the 7th day) was a scheduled day of sacred assembly. Again, the Jerusalem Christians would have been observing the prescribed sacred assembly, especially in light of the persecution they were facing. The evening following the day of sacred assembly, the Christians stayed together to pray for Peter. God dramatically intervened and delivered Peter from prison. Shortly thereafter, the Lord struck King Herod down and he died; but Peter lived to provide strong leadership for the early church (see Acts 12).

Applications in Our Day

These biblical foundations for scheduled times for revival point us to several issues churches need to address in our day.

1. **The Lord's Day.** The Lord's Day is to be kept holy and used to do good. The Christian observance of the Lord's Day needs to be a regular time to return to fellowship. We do not need the legalism of the Pharisees, but we do need a fresh call to dedicate and consecrate the day to the Lord. We need to focus special attention on the Father, His Word, and fellowship with His people. We need to avoid regular work when possible, and self-indulgent pleasure seeking. This should be a positive day of celebration and festival. It should be a day for ministry to the needy in Christ's name. It should be a day dedicated totally to the Lord.

2. **Regular Times for Renewal.** Christians need to look at the calendar to find days and times to dedicate as regular days for returning to fellowship. Certainly every observance of baptism and the Lord's Supper should bring great rejoicing, celebration, and remembering.

3. **Sacrifice and Offering.** Because of prosperity, we have forgotten the Lord. (See the warning in Deut. 6:10-12.) The tithe and proportional giving of sacrifices and offerings were instituted by God to call His people to remember God's ownership and our stewardship of all. Because of greed and disobedience, many Christians are robbing God. For these reasons, many Christians and churches are unknowingly living under the curse and wrath of God as idolaters (see Mal. 3:9; Eph. 5:5-6).

4. **Gather the People.** In sacred assemblies, all the people were gathered together. Churches may be satisfied to hold sacred assemblies with a whosoever-will-may-come attitude. God is looking for corporate repentance. Churches need to ask the Lord to direct them in ways to summon people to come together.

5. **God's Discipline.** Leaders need to be able to identify expressions of God's discipline. When discipline comes on God's people, they need to know they are being disciplined so they will respond immediately. Like Joel, leaders need to help people quickly return to the Lord.

Summary

Sacred assemblies like the one called in Joel 1–2 in response to judgment ought to be the exceptions. If regular times of renewal were faithfully observed, fellowship with God would be maintained. Today, we immediately need to respond to God's present judgments on His people and our nation by calling God's people to corporately gather before the Lord and return to Him. In the long term, we need to find regular times to accomplish the purpose of renewing fellowship with our God.

A Plumb Line for God's People can be used by God as a tool with His people. Using the Scripture as God's plumb line, you and your people can stand before God to see if you have departed from Him, and, if so, hurry back to Him in repentance.

Guiding God's People to Return to Him

The time to guide God's people to return to Him begins the moment the Holy Spirit brings conviction. This will probably be an ongoing process. Like peeling layers off an onion, God will be working to cleanse one "layer" of sin away at a time until a person and church are thoroughly clean.

Obedience to the conviction of the Holy Spirit ought to be immediate. Regardless of when and how long you have planned to use the plumb line messages, be prepared to call for confession and repentance anytime you sense God has brought His people under conviction for individual or corporate sin. This may mean canceling a sermon and giving an invitation. It might mean conducting a special service in the middle of *God's Pattern for Revival and Spiritual Awakening* for the people to respond to God. If God brings revival early, let Him do it His way! Agree with your people that you will drop your agenda and adjust to God's agenda. You do not have to wait. In fact you should not wait. God's timing always will be correct.

PRAY
Because you need to be sensitive to the Holy Spirit's leadership, you must always be in a spirit of prayer. Make prayer a primary part of your ministry. Like the apostles in Acts 6, devote yourself to prayer and the ministry of the Word. Don't allow anything to rob you of your time with God. This is such a crucial time in the life of your church, you cannot afford to miss what God is wanting to do through you. Ask your deacons or elders to assist with other duties to free you for time with God.

REVIEW CORPORATE REVIVAL EXPERIENCES IN SCRIPTURE
As preparation for planning times of corporate (group) response to God, review the revivals from Scripture that were dealt with in *God's Pattern for Revival and Spiritual Awakening*. Note the ways leaders guided the people to respond to God. You may want to go back to the Scriptures and read these revival accounts in their entirety.
- Ezra and Nehemiah (GP p. 24)
- Asa and Azariah (GP p. 66)
- Josiah and Hilkiah (GP p. 80)
- Hezekiah (GP p. 88)
- Summary (GP p. 91)

Other revival experiences that you may want to study include the revival under Samuel (see LM p. 77), the revival in Nineveh (Jonah 3), the work of Elijah on Mount Carmel (1 Kings 18:16-46), revival under Joash and Jehoiada (2 Chron. 23:16–24:15), and another revival experience under Ezra (Ezra 9–10).

T. W. Hunt has made these observations about the biblical revivals.

1. Most were preceded by high wickedness.
2. Most were attended by multiple leadership.
3. They spread from the high officials downward.
4. Previously established divine criteria were restored.
5. They were attended by great love of the written Word of God.
6. Worship, especially as expressed in the great Jewish festivals, had a primary place. It was worship from the heart.
7. The temple and the people were purified.

He adds this one sobering note. "The scriptural evidence indicates that if established leaders will not assume their God-given responsibility in revival, then God will produce new leaders in a major social upheaval."[1]

REVIEW AND REVISE YOUR USE PLAN
Review the plans you made concerning use of *A Plumb Line for God's People*. Make revisions of your plans or schedule any time you sense God's leadership in a different direction. Remain flexible and sensitive to His Spirit's leadership. Remember, this is a process to be cultivated, not a program to be completed.

PREPARE YOURSELF AND YOUR LEADERS
Continually allow God to work in your own life. As God works in you, guide other church leaders to respond to the Lord. Biblical revivals began with the leadership and moved downward. As you prepare for corporate times of renewal keep these things in mind.

Before You Pick Up the Phone. If you have a tendency to think: "I'll call Henry Blackaby or a pastor friend to get counsel for my situation," wait. Before you pick up the telephone, turn to the Lord in prayer. God wants to guide you and your church in this process. If you turn to others first, you are turning to substitutes for God, and that is a good indication that you have departed from Him. Do not, however, hesitate to seek God's counsel through other believers and particularly other leaders in your church.

Seek the Corporate Wisdom of the Body. Every member of your congregation is a priest unto the Lord. Christ is Head of your church. Christ has direct access to every leader and member. Seek the counsel of other leaders about what they sense God is saying to your church, or how He is guiding your church to respond to Him. The "eye" and the "ear" both need to be heard as the body seeks to know God's will (see 1 Cor. 12 and Rom. 12).

Trust God. What needs to take place in your church cannot happen unless it comes from God. Yes, a human response is required; but God is the one who initiates, guides, and completes His work. "Trust in the Lord with all your heart and lean not on your own understanding; in all your ways acknowledge him, and he will make your paths straight" (Prov. 3:5-6). Keep these thoughts in mind:

- In Revelation 2–3, Christ stands in the midst of His churches. Christ holds the stars (pastors) in His hand. Christ is present to help and guide the response of His people. Trust Him to be present and at work.
- Trust God to enable you to do His work, to guide your leadership. You may feel like Moses and say to God, "I can't do this. Find someone else." The truth is that apart from God you can't do anything, but with Him all things are possible. God is far more interested in bringing revival than you are. God will be present to fill you with His power and authority and work through you to accomplish what you cannot do (see Col. 1–2).
- When you recognize and are overwhelmed by your weaknesses, remember the words of Paul: "He said to me, 'My grace is sufficient for you, for my power is made perfect in weakness.' Therefore I will boast all the more gladly about my weaknesses, so that Christ's power may rest on me" (2 Cor. 12:9).
- Notice in Acts how the early churches turned to God for every problem. Follow that model.
- Remember that your job is faithfulness, not success. God is the One responsible for success, and He will measure success differently than the world does.
- Don't trust in a method, but depend on God. This ought to be good news to you. *Fresh Encounter* is a tool to guide you to God's presence. A method or program is not the answer to your needs. You do not have to know the right words to say or the right things to do. You just need God's presence and guidance. Obey Him each step of the way and you will find yourself and your church in the middle of His activity and mighty power.
- Don't substitute an outside leader for God's leadership. At some point, God may guide you to include an outside leader. However, this may be far more appropriate after revival when your church is prepared to be part of an evangelistic harvest. The Second Great Awakening (GP p. 56) is a good example of God's working primarily through pastors to bring revivals to their congregations—and those revivals impacting an entire generation!
- Don't let what you believe about your people cancel what you believe about God. Preach to the valley of dry bones (see Ezek. 37) and believe that God will bring them back to life.
- Don't be discouraged by the failure of others. Keep your eyes on God and not on the responses of the people.
- Develop and display a spirit of humility. Your dependence on God and your humility will set the tone for the response of others. The first requirement of revival is "Humble yourselves" (2 Chron. 7:14).

PREPARE THE PEOPLE

Review the suggestions under "Prepare the People for a Fresh Encounter with God" (LM p. 20). Cultivate a praying church. When God's people get close to Him in prayer and worship, like Isaiah (see Isa. 6) they will recognize a need for cleansing.

Help your people develop a sense of corporate identity. Preach about the corporate nature of the church. Emphasize the importance of the response of every member. Teach about confession and repentance.

GATHER THE PEOPLE

Ask the Lord to give you guidance about how to call the people together. Because our church members have lost their sense of corporate identity, many do not sense any accountability to the call of a church on their lives. Yet, every member needs to be involved in turning to God. The sin of one or a few can have a continuing effect on the whole body. When one member is sick, the whole body is affected.

Emphasize the importance of coming together before God to respond to Him. Help the people understand that God Himself is issuing the call to return. People may turn your invitation down. They should have greater difficulty turning down an invitation from the Lord. Remember, however, that God is the One who does the convincing. Your job is to bear witness to what you sense, and trust that God will convince members to gather together to stand before His plumb line.

REHEARSE GOD'S ACTIVITY IN YOUR CHURCH

In Deuteronomy 29, Moses gathered the people to renew their covenant with God. He began by reviewing the spiritual history of the nation to remind the people of God's faithfulness and His covenant love. Remembering the mighty activity of God in the past strengthens faith for the present.

Psalm 105 was used to help Israel remember God's activity with His people. This rehearsal of God's activity among His people in the past was a prominent part of the sacred assemblies (feast days) in Israel's history.

In Psalm 78, the writer reminds the people how seriously God treats their sin when He is acting in their behalf. The Psalmist said, "We will not hide them from their children; we will tell the next generation the praiseworthy deeds of the Lord, his power, and the wonders he has done" (Ps. 78:4).

In the revival under Ezra and Nehemiah, the leaders called the people to celebrate their past relationship with God and worship Him before they moved to repentance. Nehemiah said, "Do not grieve, for the joy of the Lord is your strength" (Neh. 8:10).

Do you remember the church at Ephesus in Revelation 2? They had left their first love. Christ commanded them: "Remember the height from which you have fallen!" (Rev. 2:5).

These illustrations from Scripture are instructive for us. Remembering where we have been with God and the "mountaintop" experiences will better prepare us for repentance and revival.

Plan a special service to rehearse God's activity with His people in your church. Celebrate the things God has done in the past. Allow those members who remember the "good old days" to tell the stories of what God did in the life of your church. Don't hide God's activity in the past from His people. Magnify it! Take time to praise and thank the Lord for all the things He has done.

Keep the focus on God's activity and not man's accomplishments. Here are some ideas that may help you celebrate.

- Ask someone to read or research your church's history and prepare a report on some of the things God has done.
- Report on missions or churches started, people called into ministry, and significant salvation experiences.
- Remember God's guidance at crucial times of decision.
- Ask for testimonies of God's special work in answer to prayer.
- Allow time for testimonies of ways people have seen God at work in the past in your church.
- Report on any significant revival experiences of the past.

Help your congregation remember where they have been with God. This will prepare them for the next steps of returning to the Lord.

IDENTIFY CORPORATE (CHURCH) SINS

Throughout your study of *God's Pattern for Revival and Spiritual Awakening*, ask leaders and members to help identify anything that may be a corporate (church) sin. Help them understand that this is a positive process that can help restore health if needed. During your leadership team meetings, ask for leaders to identify areas in which group members believe the church has sinned or departed from God.

Collect a listing of these possible sins. As pastor, gather other church leaders together. Pray together and discuss the issues that have surfaced. Compile a list of things the leaders believe are indeed sins of the church. You will want to deal with this list in a time of corporate worship. You might ask one or more leaders to read through the list of corporate sins. Call the church to confess (agree with God) their sins. Guide them in corporate prayer for repentance like that in Daniel 9, Ezra 9, or Nehemiah 9.

What are corporate sins? Any time the church has sinned by its action or lack of action, a corporate sin has been committed. Corporate sins might also include an individual sin that is common to a large number of your people (for example the intermarriage dealt with by Ezra in Ezra 9–10). Churches need to deal with all sin for which they have not repented—past and present. Examples of corporate sins might include such things as:

- participating in a church split that hindered instead of built up God's kingdom.
- adopting the ways of the world.
- allowing an ungodly person (or persons) to "run off" an innocent pastor or staff person—especially if your church has a pattern of doing so.
- choosing to do good things instead of the best things.
- coming into being as a church, group, or denomination in a wrong or sinful way: split, envy, controversy, pride.
- covering up sins of the past.
- defaulting on a debt you did not repay.
- disgracing God's name in the eyes of the community (for example a leader or member experiences moral failure that became known in the community).

- failing to care for the needs of members, families, couples.
- failing to take a strong stand for God's standards for family and marriage, and support those needing help.
- forcing agreement or compromise on a decision but with no unity of mind, heart, or spirit.
- isolating yourself from other believers, churches, and denominations in your community or state—doing your own thing when they needed your help, encouragement, or leadership.
- lacking faith when confronted with a God-sized assignment and deciding not to attempt it because of your limited resources.
- leaving a field of ministry to take the easy road (like leaving the inner city for the suburbs rather than dealing with the problems of the people in the inner city).
- making a decision contrary to God's guidance.
- mistreating pastor, staff member, or a family member.
- permitting controversy, strife, dissension.
- practicing prejudice, discrimination: poor, blacks, ethnics.
- refusing to follow God's commands related to church discipline of sinful members.
- refusing to go after the stray members who have become inactive.
- refusing to make adjustments to God because they "cost" too much.
- shifting control of the church from Christ as Head of the church to anyone else: pastor, deacons, elders, board, or power bloc in the church
- tolerating evil in the congregation.
- trying to save your life rather than give it away in service and ministry.

This is by no means a comprehensive list. Perhaps it has at least given you an idea of what is meant by corporate sin. Pay attention to the things God brings to the minds of your members. Take every suggestion seriously.

IDENTIFY DEPARTURE MARKERS

Corporate sin may include some things that took place many years ago. A small, struggling, declining church, for instance, invited a guest speaker to talk about the new church planting work being done in their area. Two different members spoke to him later, and each said something like this: "Our pastor tried to lead us to start a new church in 1954, and we refused to do it. I believe God has been punishing us for that decision ever since."

Such an event may be a "departure marker." If your members believe your church has departed from God, ask them to try to identify these departure markers. Was there an event or decision that was the beginning of the departure? If something surfaces during this search, it may help you understand what you need to do to repent, to make restitution, and to be restored.

USE THE PLUMB LINE MESSAGES

A Plumb Line for God's People is a tool God can use to help His people recognize ways they may have departed from Him. Use of the video messages and member's book does not have to be complicated. Consider the following basic format.

- Begin the service with a time of worship through singing and praying. Select music that calls people to respond to God or that is itself a response to God. The songbook, *Return to Me: A Fresh Encounter with God through Song*, offers appropriate music selections. (See the following page for more information.)
- Focus worship on God. Talk to Him. Sing to Him. Praise Him. Remember God's activity. Give God the glory due His name.
- Show the Plumb Line video message or preach on a particular topic or theme that uses God's Word as a plumb line.
- Use *A Plumb Line for God's People* member's book to help God's people examine the Scriptures further regarding the themes.
- Allow time for members to discuss in small or large groups the questions that relate to the church.
- Go beyond being Word-centered to being Christ-centered. The Word is not an end in itself. The Word points to a relationship with a Person (see John 5:39-40). The Word helps identify where a member may have departed from God. The next step is to go to God and seek to be restored to a right love relationship with Him.
- Provide a prayer room near the sanctuary. Encourage members to use the prayer room anytime during a service when they need time alone with God. If they come under conviction, that is the time to deal with God in confession and repentance. You may want to station spiritual counselors in the prayer rooms to assist people requesting help.
- Provide a time for personal and/or corporate prayer and repentance in the service.
- Invite testimonies of God's activity in the lives of believers. Follow the suggestions in "Leading a Testimony Service" on LM pages 48.

INCORPORATE APPROPRIATE MUSIC

Ron and Patricia Owens have written and/or

arranged music to support *Fresh Encounter*. The following songs go along with the listed plumb line messages and are available in the collection: *Return to Me: A Fresh Encounter with God Through Song* (see the resource listing on LM page 10).
- God's Standard for the Family: "Return to Me (family version)" and "God's Plumb Line (family)"
- Religion vs. Reality: "A New Creation" and "For Me to Live Is Christ"
- Substitutes for God: "When the Glory's Gone"
- World's Ways vs. Kingdom Ways: "Return to Me" and "Heirs to the Kingdom"
- Unholy Living vs. Holy Living: "God's Plumb Line" (verse 1), "Fullness," and "Lord of Grace and Mercy"
- Broken Relationships vs. Unity in the Body: "We Cry for Mercy, Lord" and "God's Plumb Line" (verse 2)

Songs that can be used with the phases of *God's Pattern for Revival and Spiritual Awakening* include:
- Phase 1: "God Is Looking for a People" and "God Is on Mission"
- Phase 2: "God's Plumb Line" and "When the Glory's Gone"
- Phase 3: "Lord, How Long?" and "A Jealous God"
- Phase 4: "We Cry for Mercy, Lord" and "Lord, Do It Again"
- Phase 5: "Return to Me," "If My People," and "Lord, I Repent"
- Phase 6: "Blessed Holy Spirit," "Fullness," and "Jesus Be Jesus in Me"
- Phase 7: "His Love in Me Loving," "Use Me," "Prepare the Way," and "Full Surrender"

Guide Corporate Responses

During times of corporate worship, you may need to guide corporate responses to God. Follow the basic guideline that confession ought to include the people involved and those who are aware of the sin. Remind God's people of the need for restitution and reconciliation.

Claim and confess the sins of your past. If the church becomes aware of sins that occurred years ago but have never been dealt with, guide a time of confessing for the sins of your past. See Daniel 9 for a sample prayer of confession.

Lists of corporate sins could be read and followed by prayers of confession led by spiritual leaders. A time of covenant renewal should follow. Then seek God's directions about what to do with any false idols or gods of which your church may have become aware.

Some other suggestions for corporate response include:

- Ask key people to stand, read a confession, and pray.
- Write sins on paper and nail them to a cross or burn them in a basket.
- Prepare and read a corporately written prayer and/or a written covenant.
- Provide for times of silent prayer.
- Provide for times of small- and large-group prayer.
- Offer times for simultaneous prayer.
- Invite persons to come for prayer at the altar.
- Allow members to request prayer and then immediately get an individual or group of others to pray for him or her. Utilize the members of the body.

Don't prematurely assure people of forgiveness. Allow God to bring conviction until the person realizes God is the only hope of cleansing and forgiveness.

When God restores His people, He takes them back into the mainstream of His mighty movement in history. Spiritual awakening waits for revival in the hearts of God's people. You will know revival has come when God returns to His people. Here are some evidences:
- God's presence is evident
- new freedom
- new joy
- new peace
- true worship
- a clean and clear conscience
- Christlikeness
- reconciliation (individuals, couples, families, groups, churches, denominations)
- holiness
- moral changes based on love for God, not just a reformed behavior
- ability to hear God's voice clearly
- answered prayers
- power of the Spirit evident to all
- simple authentic way of life; more like Jesus
- increased love for one another
- burden for the lost

Avoid the Dangers and Excesses of Revival

Watch for dangers of revival like physical exhaustion, inappropriate publicity, organizing the response, wrong motives, pride rather than brokenness in testimonies, emotionalism instead of encounter, activity crowding out relationship, man-centered rather than God-centered, rushed "repentance," depending on methods, and a focus on decision rather than conversion.

---
[1] Taken from "Christ-Centered Revival" in *National Prayer Conference Notebook*, June 1990, p. 11.

NOTES

Leading a Testimony Service

[Contributed by Bill Elliff, pastor, Little Rock, Arkansas]

One of the primary ingredients for the spread of historic revivals has been an abundance of personal testimonies. The accounting of the work of God in individual hearts can prove a powerful tool in the hands of God to inspire, encourage, and convict others of their need.

COMMON FEARS REGARDING TESTIMONY TIMES

Often pastors are fearful of testimony times for the following reasons.

- Embarrassingly "dry" testimonies.
- Excessively long or emotional testimonies.
- Testimonies that step over certain lines of propriety.
- Nonspecific, generalized testimonies that seem useless and unedifying.

THE VALUE OF A TESTIMONY TIME

Testimonies can provide freedom for God to accomplish manifold good in the following ways.

1. Give God the glory due Him as He has transformed lives.
2. Help believers confirm and verbalize what God is doing in their lives.
3. Allow specific testimonies to inspire, convict, encourage, teach, and train other believers.
4. Grow the church through a fresh sense of the magnitude of corporate work God is doing in the body of Christ.
5. Give the pastor an opportunity to identify and preach from certain primary themes that are repeatedly identified during testimonies.
6. Provide a spiritual thermometer by giving church leaders an increased understanding of where God is at work and by identifying primary areas of need.
7. Give opportunity for public confession and corporate forgiveness when needed.

HINTS FOR LEADING AN EFFECTIVE TESTIMONY TIME

The following are hints on how to lead an effective testimony time. The average lay person may be just as fearful regarding these times as a pastor, often because of bad experiences in the past. Ruling out these fears by proper explanation in advance can pave the way for a fresh release of God's Spirit.

◆ Pray! Spend time privately and publicly praying for:

- God to convince just the right people to share.
- Protection from the enemy.
- Wisdom, as the pastor, to know how to lead the time—particularly how to be sensitive to key points of conviction.

◆ Take time to educate the congregation on how to give a testimony. The following model might be used.

a. Share how God is developing in each Christian a special life message that is peculiar to her. God is using all the experiences of a Christian's life and the right responses to develop these truths in them. Learning to clearly articulate and transparently communicate these truths to others is one of the great keys in usefulness for God's kingdom.

b. Describe how to share a life message (you may want to put these on an overhead projector or a simple handout.)

   1. Share where God found you. Be specific regarding areas of sin, need, and so on.
   2. Share what you were experiencing as a result of controlling your own life.
   3. Share what God said to you.
   4. Share how you responded. You may have responded negatively at first. Be honest.
   5. Share what you are now experiencing as a result of obedience to God's truth. What benefits of obedience are you experiencing?

c. Describe simple ground rules.

   1. Be brief.
   2. Be specific.
   3. Be current.
   4. Bring all the glory to God.
   5. Don't reflect negatively on others.
   6. Use the term "moral failure" for any moral sins.

d. Invite the congregation to think of one area where God has been working in recent days (you may want to identify this as the past week, month, six months, for example). Then ask them to turn to one other person and, using the above method, share a brief three-minute testimony.

e. Spend a moment in prayer. Let them ask God whether He wants them to share a public testimony. Invite those who feel so led to come forward. Indicate that you may or may not get to all who came forward. This gives the pastor the discretion to choose those to whom he feels led.

f. As they come, the pastor can stand by those who are sharing. Feel free to interrupt and help them clarify or give further specifics if needed. Offer encouragement and love.

g. Lead in ministering to the person after he has shared.

   1. Give a word of encouragement or affirmation if appropriate.
   2. If he has asked for the church's forgiveness, lead the church in corporately verbalizing "I forgive you!" to the individual.
   3. Invite people to give a hug or a word to those testifying as they head back to their seats.
   4. If the testifier still has needs or burdens, invite a group of people with concerned hearts to gather around that person or take them to a side room for prayer, encouragement, or counsel as needed.

h. Be sensitive not only to the person testifying, but to what God is saying to the church through the testimonies. Remind the people that they are not spectators but participants in this time. God may be speaking directly to them about similar or related issues. When a similar testimony is repeated several times, see this as God speaking to the church.

i. Be sensitive to opportunities to preach from the subjects raised in testimonies. Don't feel the need to say something after every testimony. If God brings to your mind key thoughts that will help crystallize and convict through the testimonies, seize the opportunity, perhaps even stop for an invitation.

OTHER HELPFUL HINTS

1. Don't worry about excesses. If someone seems to step over the line in some way, thank God publicly that people feel the freedom to share, then gently remind them of the boundaries for the testimonies.
2. When people share things that should have been shared with another individual, ask them to go to that individual immediately if possible to clear their conscience.
3. Don't feel you must have everyone share. It is often better to stop on a significant note instead of prolonging the testimony time. This leaves the congregation anxious to hear more from God. Inform those who did not get to share that there will be other opportunities, and affirm their obedience to God in being willing to share.
4. Remind people often that every testimony is significant.

Although these suggestions may seem mechanical, they have proven helpful to many pastors in aiding believers to express God's activity in their lives. Trust God to use you in opening the way of blessing through this wonderful, biblical practice.

Continuing Renewal

Once revival comes, we need to institute periodic times of renewal that will help us regularly return to the Lord. By doing so, we should not get so far away from Him. The following are some suggestions God can use with His people to continue renewal.

HOLY DAYS

Christian holy days (holidays) like Christmas and Easter ought to be times of renewal. On these days, place your focus on both celebration and renewal of a relationship. These are days to remember all the love God has lavished on us by sending His Son. Rather than go through time-honored traditions as mere ritual, these can be times for remembering God's love and responding to that love. They can be times to call for repentance.

PRECOMMUNION MEETINGS

In the past century, and among some groups today, precommunion meetings have been used as a time for repentance. On the Saturday prior to the Sunday observance of the Lord's Supper, an entire congregation sets aside all regular work and comes together for a time of examination. The time is used for the people to confess and repent of all known sin and correct broken relationships, lest they partake of the Lord's Supper in an unworthy state (see 1 Cor. 11:27-32). They do everything possible to have clean hands, pure hearts, and clear consciences before God as they come to the Lord's table.

Restoring meaning and purpose to the observance of the Lord's Supper would help in continuing renewal. Regularly providing time for members to examine themselves and repent of all known sin could be a valuable measure to keep us close to the Lord.

PENTECOST PRAYER MEETINGS

In *The Prayer Life*, Andrew Murray describes the beginning of Pentecost prayer meetings. The revival of 1857–58 in America spread to South Africa by 1860. In 1861 the pastors decided to hold prayer meetings in the afternoons one week prior to Pentecost. Many hearts were warmed and deeply touched.

Since Pentecost has special significance for the coming of the Holy Spirit on the church, churches decided to spend the 10 days between Ascension and Pentecost observing daily prayer like the disciples in the upper room. Over the next 50 years the Pentecost prayer meetings were observed. Pastors circulated notes with subjects for sermons and prayer.

According to Murray, these prayer meetings frequently were times of revival for God's people. He said they often were followed by fruitful evangelistic harvests. You might want to consider some special prayer meetings leading up to Pentecost.

PILGRIM PRAYER MEETINGS

In 1816 in Wales, William Williams was preaching about the work of the Holy Spirit. He offered this suggestion to the parish:

> "What if you were to consent to have Him to save the whole of this parish? 'Ah, but how can we have Him?' Well, hold prayer-meetings through the whole parish; go from house to house—every house that will open its door. Make it the burden of every prayer that God should come here to save. If God has not come by the time you have gone through the parish once, go through it again; but if you are in earnest in your prayers, you shall not go through half the parish before God has come to you."[1]

In that service was a lonely old woman with little religious background. Though very poor, she splurged and bought two wax candles to be ready for the pilgrim prayer meeting when it came to her house. Almost a year later, the discouraged woman went to the shop where she had bought the candles. She asked the owner when the prayer meeting was coming to her house. The owner felt rebuked, for none of the church members had taken the suggestion seriously. He reported the incident to the church and the pilgrim prayer meetings began.

Your church might consider having pilgrim prayer meetings, moving from house to house praying for each family of your church and community until God sends revival.

BODY LIFE MEETINGS

The church is described as the body of Christ. Every member has an important role in helping the body function properly. A Body Life meeting is a time for members of the body to care for and strengthen one another. It can be a time for testimonies, for sharing special prayer requests, for praying for each other, for rejoicing with those who rejoice, and for weeping with those who weep. It can be a time for members to share faults, weaknesses, or needs and have the rest of the body minister to the ones in need.

A Body Life meeting is a time of corporate worship and sharing that is more informal and intimate than a traditional service. Consider planning a service around the idea of "Body Life." Ask members to study Romans 12 and 1 Corinthians 12, making a list of ways the members of the body of Christ relate to one another. Encourage members to share needs, request prayer, testify to God's goodness, remember God's blessings in the past, and discuss ways to help and encourage one another. You might use the "Body Life Meeting" worksheet on LM page 54 to get members thinking about how they can "spur one another on toward love and good deeds" (Heb. 10:24).

TESTIMONY MEETINGS

Using the suggestions for "Leading a Testimony Service" on LM page 48, provide regular times for God's people to declare His marvelous deeds among the people (see Psalm 96). God uses testimonies of His recent activity in one person's life to create a desire in another person for a similar experience with Him. As people hear of God's activity, their faith is increased and they trust God to work in their lives and families.

CLEANSING BY WASHING WITH WATER THROUGH THE WORD

The activities by this title in *God's Pattern for Revival and Spiritual Awakening* can serve as a model God can use in helping people to constantly hold their lives up against the plumb line of His Word. Present Scriptures related to a particular theme in a bulletin insert. Read them from the pulpit or guide the congregation in a responsive reading. Present a choral reading of Scriptures.

The Scriptures are not an end in themselves. They should always be pointing people to a relationship. Therefore, ask people to reflect on those Scriptures or respond to God in some way. For instance, after the presentation of Scriptures, ask:
- What would God want you to do in response to this truth?
- Is God convicting you of any sin? Then confess it and return to Him.
- Get in small groups of four or five people who are close by you. Pray sentence prayers of thanksgiving for what God has done for you.

On occasion you might take a more extended period of time to deal with Scripture. The "Love = Obedience" worksheet (LM p. 55) could be distributed following a message on the relationship between love and obedience. Ask members to read the list of sins and related Scriptures of their choosing during the coming week. Encourage them to seek the Holy Spirit's conviction for any sin with which they need to deal.

PREPARING YOUR OWN PLUMB LINE MESSAGES

Use the activities in *A Plumb Line for God's People* as a model for preparing your own messages. Let God identify a subject He wants to deal with in your congregation. Provide a listing of Scriptures with appropriate questions or activities to help people evaluate their lives against God's plumb line on the given subject. Preach or teach on the subject. Call people to respond to God and return in any area where they recognize a departure from Him.

CHURCH DISCIPLINE

God holds every individual accountable for his own sin. He expects us to respond to the conviction of the Holy Spirit in dealing with individual sin. If a Christian refuses to deal with his own sin, God intends for the church to deal with it. A church is made up of many members, but they are one body. If one member is living in rebellion, the whole body is accountable.

Church discipline must be undertaken in a careful, loving, and God-directed manner. When the early church disciplined wayward members, great fear came on the people that increased their level of faithfulness. God has commanded the church to deal with sin in the church. When we fail to take God-prescribed action, the church sins and invites God's discipline.

You probably will need to prepare your church for such a step. Because of former abuses of church discipline, we have departed from the clear commands of the Lord. Careful teaching and much prayer will be required for a church to let God guide them in this practice.

What are some of the things God says about church discipline? Read the Scripture on the next page to discover what God says.

Romans 14:12 • Each of us will give an account of himself to God.

1 Corinthians 12:25-26 • [25]There should be no division in the body, but that its parts should have equal concern for each other. [26]If one part suffers, every part suffers with it; if one part is honored, every part rejoices with it.

Galatians 6:1-2 • [1]Brothers, if someone is caught in a sin, you who are spiritual should restore him gently. But watch yourself, or you also may be tempted. [2]Carry each other's burdens, and in this way you will fulfill the law of Christ.

James 5:19-20 • [19]My brothers, if one of you should wander from the truth and someone should bring him back, [20]remember this: Whoever turns a sinner from the error of his way will save him from death and cover over a multitude of sins.

1 Timothy 5:19-21 • [19]Do not entertain an accusation against an elder unless it is brought by two or three witnesses. [20]Those who sin are to be rebuked publicly, so that the others may take warning.

[21]I charge you, in the sight of God and Christ Jesus and the elect angels, to keep these instructions without partiality, and to do nothing out of favoritism.

Titus 3:10 • Warn a divisive person once, and then warn him a second time. After that, have nothing to do with him.

2 Timothy 4:2 • Preach the Word; be prepared in season and out of season; correct, rebuke and encourage—with great patience and careful instruction.

2 Thessalonians 3:14-15 • [14]If anyone does not obey our instruction in this letter, take special note of him. Do not associate with him in order that he may feel ashamed. [15]Yet do not regard him as an enemy, but warn him as a brother.

1 Thessalonians 5:14-18 • [14]We urge you, brothers, warn those who are idle, encourage the timid, help the weak, be patient with everyone. [15]Make sure that nobody pays back wrong for wrong, but always try to be kind to each other and to everyone else.

[16]Be joyful always; [17]pray continually; [18]give thanks in all circumstances, for this is God's will for you in Christ Jesus.

1 Corinthians 5:6-7,9-13 • [6]Don't you know that a little yeast works through the whole batch of dough? [7]Get rid of the old yeast that you may be a new batch without yeast. . . . [9]I have written you in my letter not to associate with sexually immoral people—[10]not at all meaning the people of this world who are immoral. . . . In that case you would have to leave this world. [11]But now I am writing you that you must not associate with anyone who calls himself a brother but is sexually immoral or greedy, an idolater or a slanderer, a drunkard or a swindler. With such a man do not even eat.

[12]What business is it of mine to judge those outside the church? Are you not to judge those inside? [13]God will judge those outside. "Expel the wicked man from among you."

2 Corinthians 7:8-11 • [8]I see that my letter hurt you . . . [9]now I am happy, not because you were made sorry, but because your sorrow led you to repentance. . . . [10]Godly sorrow brings repentance that leads to salvation and leaves no regret, but worldly sorrow brings death. [11]See what this godly sorrow has produced in you: what earnestness, what eagerness to clear yourselves, what indignation, what alarm, what longing, what concern, what readiness to see justice done.

2 Corinthians 13:1 • "Every matter must be established by the testimony of two or three witnesses."

Other Ideas for Continuing Renewal
- God Watch—Encourage people to watch for God's activity around your church and community and then report to the body.
- Discipleship Training—When a life is swept clean and not filled with a new way of living, old patterns may return (see Matt. 12:43-45). Provide training in right living to fill the void left by cleansing of a life.
- House of Prayer—Make every effort to develop a praying church. Don't focus on the activity of

prayer but on the relationship to the Lord of the universe.
- Restore Meaning to Worship—Many practices of worship have lost their meaning. We have a tendency to treat them as common or as mere ritual. Baptism and the Lord's Supper services ought to be significant times of worship. [You may want to secure helps like: "Baptismal Manual: Making Baptism More Meaningful" by Gerald Steffy, Metro Peoria Association, 2018 N. Wisconsin Ave., Peoria, IL 61603.]

[1] From *Glory Filled the Land* edited by Richard Owen Roberts, p. 20.

IDEAS FOR CONTINUING RENEWAL

Body Life Meeting

ENCOURAGE ONE ANOTHER

Divide into groups of three. Read Hebrews 10:19-25. As you read, underline or circle answers to the following questions.

1. What has God done to prepare the way for us to enter His presence?

2. What can we do to help each other as we prepare for the coming of the Lord?

Hebrews 10:19-25 • [19]Brothers, since we have confidence to enter the Most Holy Place by the blood of Jesus, [20]by a new and living way opened for us through the curtain, that is, his body, [21]and since we have a great priest over the house of God, [22]let us draw near to God with a sincere heart in full assurance of faith, having our hearts sprinkled to cleanse us from a guilty conscience and having our bodies washed with pure water. [23]Let us hold unswervingly to the hope we profess, for he who promised is faithful. [24]And let us consider how we may spur one another on toward love and good deeds. [25]Let us not give up meeting together, as some are in the habit of doing, but let us encourage one another—and all the more as you see the Day approaching.

After you have discussed and answered the two questions above, answer the following questions on applying these instructions to the body life of your church.

3. In what ways can we encourage each other toward love and good deeds?

4. Do we need to change our habits of meeting together with other believers for mutual encouragement? If so, how?

5. What major adjustments will be required for us to live this way?

Close your sharing time by praying for one another.

© LifeWay Press, 1993. Used by permission.

* You have permission to reproduce this worksheet from *Fresh Encounter Leader's Manual* for use in your church or group.

Biblical quotations are taken from the Holy Bible, *New International Version*, copyright © 1973, 1978, 1984 by International Bible Society.

Love = Obedience

According to Jesus, disobedience (or sin) indicates that you do not love Him the way you need to love Him. Jesus said: "If you love me, you will obey what I command. . . . Whoever has my commands and obeys them, he is the one who loves me. . . . He who does not love me will not obey my teaching" (John 14:15,21,24). Obedience comes from a love relationship with God. Disobedience is a sign that you have a problem in your love relationship with God. You need to return to an intimate love relationship with God.

No one could number the ways a person can sin against God. Many words in the Bible relate to what we commonly call sin. We sin against God when we:
- miss the mark of His purposes for us,
- rebel against Him, refuse to follow Him, and
- commit acts of evil, wickedness, or immorality.

We may become so disoriented to God, however, that we do not recognize our sinful ways. The following list may help you think through your life and perhaps identify things in your life that are displeasing to God. One job of the Holy Spirit is to convict of sin. Ask Him to call attention to any of the following areas that may indicate an obedience problem.

God is interested in a broken heart that confesses and repents of sin. However, more than turning away from sin, God wants you to turn to Him and have an intimate love relationship with Him. God does not want you to settle for feeling guilty and not changing. Do not, however, let Satan accuse you of sins God has already forgiven. Once forgiven, you will experience the joy of your salvation.

Ask the Holy Spirit to reveal to you any of the following sins of which you are guilty. Let Him call you back to a fresh new love of your Heavenly Father.

Ephesians 5:3-6
Idolatry of the heart
- sexual immorality
- impurity
- greed

Ephesians 5:4
- obscenity
- foolish talk
- coarse joking

James 4:11
- slandering one another (brothers)
- speaking against a brother, judging a brother

James 5:1-9
- hoarding wealth in the last days
- failing to pay workers
- condemning innocent men
- grumbling against one another

1 Corinthians 10:1-13
- setting your hearts on evil things
- idolatry
- sexual immorality
- testing the Lord
- grumbling

Mark 7:21-23
- evil thoughts
- theft
- adultery
- malice
- lewdness
- slander
- folly
- sexual immorality
- murder
- greed
- deceit
- envy
- arrogance

Matthew 5:21-37
- murder, angry with brother without cause
- adultery, looking at a woman lustfully
- frivolous divorce
- swearing an oath

2 Peter 3:3-4
- scoffers
- following own evil desires
- scoffing about the second coming of Christ

2 Timothy 3:1-5
- lovers of self
- lovers of money
- boastful
- proud
- abusive
- disobedient to parents
- ungrateful
- unholy
- without love
- unforgiving
- slanderous

- without self-control
- brutal
- not lovers of good
- treacherous
- rash
- conceited
- lovers of pleasure rather than lovers of God
- having a form of godliness but denying its power

REVELATION 2–3
Churches that:
- have forsaken their first love
- entice others to sin through idolatry and immorality
- tolerate those who practice immorality, idolatry, and false teaching
- have the reputation of being alive but are dead
- are neither cold nor hot
- have allowed prosperity and success to blind them of their need for God

DEUTERONOMY 27:15-26
Cursed is the man who . . .
- carves an image or casts an idol
- dishonors his father or mother
- moves his neighbor's boundary stone
- leads the blind astray
- withholds justice from the alien, the fatherless, or the widow
- sleeps with his father's wife
- has sexual relations with an animal
- sleeps with his sister
- sleeps with his mother-in-law
- kills his neighbor secretly
- accepts a bribe to kill an innocent person
- does not uphold the words of this law by carrying them out

EZEKIEL 18
- defiles his neighbor's wife
- oppresses the poor and needy
- commits robbery
- lends at usury and takes excessive interest

PROVERBS 6:16-19
- haughty eyes
- a lying tongue
- hands that shed innocent blood
- a heart that devises wicked schemes
- feet that are quick to rush into evil
- a false witness
- a man who stirs up dissension among brothers

OTHERS
- a gossip who betrays a confidence (Prov. 11:13)
- blasphemy of the Holy Spirit (Mark 3:29)
- deceiving a neighbor about something left to his care (Lev. 6:1)
- dishonesty through use of inaccurate weights and measures (Deut. 25:14, 16)
- prophets who say they have a word from the Lord and prophesy peace when there is no peace (Ezek. 13:10)
- partaking of the Lord's supper in an unworthy manner (1 Cor. 11:27)
- saying we have not sinned (1 John 1:8)
- friendship with the world (Jas. 4:4-5)
- honoring God with the lips while the heart is far from God (Mark 7:6)
- if a person does not speak up when he hears a public charge to testify regarding something he has seen or learned about (Lev. 5:1)
- injustice (Ps. 58:2)
- letting go of the commands of God and holding to the traditions of man (Mark 7:8)
- not keeping the Sabbath Day (Lord's Day) holy to the Lord (Ex. 20:8-11)
- presumption—presuming on the will of God without a word from God (Num. 14:44)
- religious leaders who do not practice what they preach — they put heavy loads on men's shoulders and are not willing to lift a finger to move them (Matt. 23:3-4)
- robbing God of the tithe (Mal. 3:6-9)
- refusing to follow God wholeheartedly (Num. 32:11)

© LifeWay Press, 1993. Used by permission.
* You have permission to reproduce this worksheet from *Fresh Encounter Leader's Manual* for use in your church or group.

Biblical quotations are taken from the Holy Bible, *New International Version,* copyright © 1973, 1978, 1984 by International Bible Society.

Guiding a Study of God's Pattern for Revival and Spiritual Awakening

This section of the *Leader's Manual* is for leaders who will be guiding the small-group study of *God's Pattern for Revival and Spiritual Awakening*. Pastors and key leaders should be a vital part of the small-group experience with God. Remember, this is not just a course; it is an encounter with Holy God.

> **SMALL-GROUP LEADER'S PREPARATION CHECKLIST**
>
> Complete the items in the following checklist as a guide for your preparation to lead a study of *God's Pattern for Revival and Spiritual Awakening*.
> ❑ 1. Pray that the Lord clearly will prepare and guide you as you lead this study of *God's Pattern for Revival and Spiritual Awakening*.
> ❑ 2. Attend the orientation for *God's Pattern* small-group leaders.
> ❑ 3. Study *God's Pattern for Revival and Spiritual Awakening*. This may be completed week by week as you study along with your group members.
> ❑ 4. Read these parts of *Fresh Encounter Leader's Manual*.
>   ❑ How to Use this Manual (p. 7)
>   ❑ Overview of *Fresh Encounter* (p. 8)
>   ❑ Warning! (p. 11)
>   ❑ Getting Ready for a *Fresh Encounter* with God (p. 14)
>   ❑ Needed: Spiritual Leaders (p. 23)
>   ❑ Guiding a Study of *God's Pattern for Revival and Spiritual Awakening* (p. 57)
>   ❑ Session Plans for *God's Pattern for Revival and Spiritual Awakening* (p. 64)

USING THE SESSION PLANS FOR GOD'S PATTERN

The session plans (beginning on LM page 64) will assist you in preparing for and conducting the small-group sessions for *God's Pattern for Revival and Spiritual Awakening*. Remember to be person-centered and God-centered and not method- or content-centered in your planning. The plans provide an introductory session and six weekly sessions. The introductory session may be used in small groups, several large groups, or an entire congregation, depending on the size of your church. The six session plans are designed for use in small groups of six to ten people.

If you want to save time, much of the preparation for weekly sessions can be completed at one time prior to starting the course. For suggestions for advanced planning see "Prepare or Secure Resources" on the next page. Some of this material is optional. You will also find that more suggestions are given in the session plans than you will be able to complete in a 60- to 90-minute session. You may want to read through session plans and determine which activities you plan to use before securing additional resources.

LM pages 64–117 provide step-by-step procedures for conducting the group sessions. Each session plan includes three parts.

Before the Session. This section includes actions for you to complete before the group session. Boxes (❑) are provided for you to check as you complete each action. We have tried to provide session plans that require a minimum of preparation so you can give yourself to prayer and personal spiritual preparation.

During the Session. This section provides learning activities for you to use in conducting a 60- to 90-minute small-group session. The activities follow a similar pattern each week. For many groups, the plans provide more activities than can be completed in this period of time. The reason we have provided so much is to give a leader flexibility in customizing the session for his or her particular group. You will want use the most important or helpful activities first. Don't get frustrated if you do not get to all the activities. The primary goal of these study times is to help people understand God's pattern for revival and spiritual awakening. Groups and individuals can review or dig deeper into the study at a later time if they sense the need for more insight. Again, remember the danger of focusing on activities completed rather than on the love relationship encountered.

After the Session. This section guides you in evaluating the group session, your sensitivity as a leader, and the needs of group members. This evaluation will help you improve your ability to guide the group in their fresh encounter with God. It will also help you process what God is saying to your group for sharing in the leadership team meetings.

Your Role as a Small-Group Leader

Your role in a small-group study of *God's Pattern for Revival and Spiritual Awakening* is not that of a teacher. You are a facilitator of the group learning process, a spiritual catalyst in the midst of God's presence. If you sense God has called you to this assignment, you can use activities to equip and enable you to accomplish the task. You are an instrument—a servant—through whom God wants to do His work. Your greatest responsibility is to depend on God for direction.

Group members will be spending time each week studying the content in the member's book. The Holy Spirit is going to be their Teacher; He will be your Teacher, too. The content and learning activities will help members learn the basic Bible truths and encounter God during the week. Your job is to (1) help them review what they have learned; (2) share with each other what God has revealed about themselves and their relationship to Him; (3) discuss what God has revealed about their relationship to Him corporately as His church; and (4) apply these truths to their personal lives, their families, their work, and to their church's life as a love relationship with God on mission in their world.

Prepare or Secure Resources

You will need to secure or prepare the following resources for use in the sessions. In some cases these resources may be provided by the *Fresh Encounter* facilitator or some other person in your church. Some churches will provide copies of the worksheets for all groups. Check with your church before making copies for yourself. The following list describes every item you will need for the study that is not included in the member's books. Once you have secured or prepared the following resources, you have all the materials you will need.

- ❑ A Bible
- ❑ Provide copies of Fresh Encounter: God's Pattern for Revival and Spiritual Awakening for each member of your group.
- ❑ Provide for each group member a photocopy of the following worksheets:
  - ❑ Introducing God's Pattern (LM p. 69)
  - ❑ Revival Under Samuel (LM p. 77)
  - ❑ God at Work (LM p. 84)
  - ❑ Heart Idols (LM p. 92)
  - ❑ God Judged Judah for Its Sin (LM p.102)
  - ❑ Penalties for Disobedience (LM p. 103)
  - ❑ Your First Love (LM p. 109)
- ❑ Optional: one copy of "Pray for Revival in the Land" (LM p. 61) for use in the introductory session.
- ❑ One photocopy of "Asbury Revival Testimonies" (LM pp. 116–117) for use in Session 6.
- ❑ Make the poster described on LM page 64. You may want to laminate it or cover it with clear plastic adhesive shelf paper for durability.
- ❑ Provide poster board or newsprint and markers for Session 1.
- ❑ Cut out the diagrams on LM pages 85 and 86 for Session 2. You may want to laminate them or cover them with clear plastic adhesive shelf paper.
- ❑ Prepare the poster in "Before the Session" for Session 2. (LM p. 80).
- ❑ Cut out and laminate the diagrams (LM pp. 93–96) for session 3 before the session.

Help Members Memorize Scripture

Some of your group members may not be skilled at memorizing Scripture. The following suggestions may be helpful. Write the boldface instructions on a poster for use in the introductory and first small-group session. Be prepared to explain each of the suggestions.

Memorizing Scripture

1. **Write the verse and reference on an index card.**
2. **Seek understanding.** Read the verse in its context. For instance, for 2 Chronicles 7:14 you might read 2 Chronicles 6–7. Study the verse and try to understand what it means.
3. **Read the verse aloud several times.**
4. **Learn to quote the verse.** Divide the verse into short and meaningful phrases. Learn to quote the first phrase word for word. Then build on it by learning the second phrase. Continue until you are able to quote the entire verse word for word.
5. **Repeat the verse to another person and ask him or her to check your accuracy.**
6. **Review the memorized verse regularly.** During the first week, carry the card in your pocket or purse. Pull it out for review several times daily during waiting periods—like riding an elevator, riding to work, or taking a coffee or lunch break. Review the verse at least daily for the first six weeks. Review weekly for the next six weeks and monthly thereafter.
7. **Remember, memorizing Scripture is an encounter with a Person.** "Jesus answered, 'I am the way and the truth and the life' " (John 14:6).

ENCOURAGE MEMBERS TO KEEP A JOURNAL

Some people may want to write down responses to questions for reflection in "Encountering God in Prayer" and in other sections. God will be dealing with people in a variety of ways.

A journal will provide space for recording prayers and listing prayer requests, answers to prayer, responses to reflection questions, and responses to "Encountering God in Prayer." The journal also will provide for recording what the person senses God is saying to him or her through His Word and in times of prayer. The journal could be a place to keep a "to do" list of things a person senses God wants to happen in response to the study.

Sometimes responses to questions in the member's book may be too personal or confidential for a person to feel free to record them where someone might see them. The journal would be a good place for recording these personal responses for future reference, meditation, or prayer.

Tell members that they do not need to feel under pressure to write something every day. The journal is for their personal use.

ANSWERING HARD QUESTIONS

Group members may ask some hard questions that you cannot answer. When you do not know the answer (or maybe even when you do), encourage the group to join you in praying and searching the Scriptures. Together, ask God to guide you to His answer, to His perspective. Then trust God to do it. You also may want to write the question down and share it during the leadership team meeting.

RESPONDING TO GOD'S ACTIVITY IN A GROUP

One of the lessons you need to learn from the Lord is how to respond to God's activity in a group experience. Normally, we have not been taught how to respond when God interrupts our group activities, plans, or programs. This is a lesson God can and will teach you. You can depend on Him. He cares far more for your group than you do. If He wants to work in the midst of that group in a special way, He can and will enable you to respond appropriately. However, you must make some prior commitments in the way you function as a spiritual leader. You must give your plans and agenda to God. If He interrupts your group, cancel your agenda and see what God wants to do.

We were leading a conference for 150 people. Small groups were just completing a sharing and prayer time. Henry was to speak next. A woman stood and explained that one of the women in her group needed us to pray for her. The woman had been abused as a young child and now her father was at home dying from cancer. She was having trouble coming to terms with her father's death.

We have seen God bring dramatic emotional and spiritual healing to people like her. We realized God wanted to do more than just share a prayer request with our group. We had to decide to pray briefly and go on with our teaching agenda or turn the session over to God. We had already agreed before the conference that if God ever interrupted us we would cancel our agenda and give Him freedom to work. That is what we did.

We knew that God had entrusted that woman's needs to this group, so we assumed that He also had placed in that group the people who could best minister to her. We asked those who could identify with her need to come and stand around her and pray with her. Eight or ten women came to minister to her in prayer. We then gave an invitation for others to come for prayer if they had deep needs that only God could meet. People led by God then came to pray with those who responded.

As God completed His work in a person's life, we gave him or her an opportunity to share with the group what God had done. Often the testimony would be used of God to invite someone with a similar problem to come to Him to be set free. For the rest of the hour we watched as God used members of that group to minister to other members who had needs. People who had been in spiritual bondage for decades found freedom in Christ. Others experienced the comfort, healing, and peace that only God can give. Some for the first time in their lives experienced (and felt) the love of a Father—a Heavenly Father. Those who were used of God in ministry to others experienced God working through them in dramatic ways. We learned more about God in that hour through experience than we could have learned in a week of lectures.

Here are some suggestions for responding to God's activity in your group.

- Spend much time in developing your personal relationship with God so that you come to know the voice of God when He is speaking to you.
- If you have not already done so, study *Experiencing God: Knowing and Doing the Will of God*. This course will help you identify God's activity around you. It will help you learn to know God's voice when He is speaking to you. It will help you recognize God's invitations for you to join Him.

- Before group sessions, take time to be sure all sins have been confessed and you have a clear conscience before God.
- Place your absolute trust in God to guide you when He wants to work in your group setting.
- Decide beforehand that you will cancel your agenda and give God freedom to move anytime He shows you that He wants to do a special work. When you see God at work in your group, that is your invitation as a leader to join Him. The primary purpose of this time is to encounter God, not just cover the material.
- Watch for things like tears of joy or conviction, emotional or spiritual brokenness, the thrill of a newfound insight, or a desire for prayer in response to a need. These things are sometimes seen only on a facial expression or heard in a quiet sigh. Determine whether you need to talk to the person with the group or privately. You must depend on the Holy Spirit for such guidance.
- Respond by asking a probing question like one of these: Is something happening in your life right now that you would share with us? How can we pray for you? Would you share with us what God is doing in your life? What can we do to be of help to you?
- If the person responds by sharing, then provide ministry based on the need. If he does not seem ready to respond, do not push or pressure him. Give God time to work in the person's life.
- When appropriate, invite members to share in ministry to one another. This may be to pray, to comfort, to counsel privately, or to rejoice with the person. When you do not feel equipped to deal with a problem that surfaces, ask the group if one of them feels led to help. You will be amazed how God works to provide just the right person to give the needed ministry. The corporate life of God's people is crucial.
- Give people the opportunity to testify to what God is doing. This is a critical point. Often the testimony of one person may be used of God to help another person with a similar problem or challenge. Hearing testimony of God's wonderful work is also one of the best ways for people to experience God. Do not hide God's glory from His people when God is clearly at work in your group.
- When you do not sense a clear direction about what to do next, ask the group. Say something like "I do not have a clear sense of what we need to do next. Does anyone have a sense of what God would want us to do?"
- Continue on God's agenda until you feel He is finished with you. The encounter will be real.

We cannot give you directions for handling every situation. But we can speak from experience: When God wants to work in a group, He can and will give the guidance needed for that time. Your job is to recognize His voice and do everything you sense He wants you to do. At the same time, trust Him to work through His body—the church. He has placed members in your group and gifted them to build up the body of Christ. Acknowledge and use all of the resources God has given your group.

Pray for Revival in the Land

Our Sovereign God is the ruler of men and nations. Throughout history He has established nations, and poured out His wrath and judgment on nations that depart from Him and live in wickedness. If our nation is to survive, we must turn to the Lord our God. God alone is our Hope. We must trust in Him.

Psalm 33:10-22 •

¹⁰The Lord foils the plans of the nations;
   he thwarts the purposes of the peoples.
¹¹But the plans of the Lord stand firm forever,
   the purposes of his heart through all
      generations.
¹²Blessed is the nation whose God is the
   Lord,
 the people he chose for his inheritance.
¹³From heaven the Lord looks down and
   sees all mankind;
¹⁴from his dwelling place he watches all who
   live on earth—
¹⁵he who forms the hearts of all,
   who considers everything they do.
¹⁶No king is saved by the size of his army;
   no warrior escapes by his great
      strength.
¹⁷A horse is a vain hope for deliverance;
   despite all its great strength it cannot
      save.
¹⁸But the eyes of the Lord are on those who
   fear him,
   on those whose hope is in his unfailing
      love,
¹⁹to deliver them from death and keep them
   alive in famine.
²⁰We wait in hope for the Lord;
   he is our help and our shield.
²¹In him our hearts rejoice,
   for we trust in his holy name.
²²May your unfailing love rest upon us,
   O Lord,
 even as we put our hope in you.

Many sense that the problems faced by our nation today are the consequences of our sin and the evidence of the discipline and judgment of God. If our nation is to return to the Lord and fear Him once again, God's people must take the lead. The healing of our land is waiting for the repentance and revival of God's people.

2 Chronicles 7:14 • "If my people, who are called by my name, will humble themselves and pray and seek my face and turn from their wicked ways, then will I hear from heaven and will forgive their sin and will heal their land."

The following is an example from history where a leader called his nation to repent. The leadership sensed the Civil War they faced was the result of God's discipline for the nation's sins. Though the division of the nation was great, the war came to an end; the nation was reunited; and the land was healed.

A Nation Repents

During the period of the Civil War in the United States, both houses of Congress and President Abraham Lincoln sensed a desperate need for the nation to humble themselves before Almighty God and confess their sins and repent before Him. The following excerpts come from proclamations issued by President Lincoln between 1861 and 1864.

Proclamation of a National Fast Day August 12, 1861

"Whereas a joint committee of both houses of Congress has waited on the President of the United States and requested him to 'recommend a day of public prayer, humiliation, and fasting, to be observed by the people of the United States with religious solemnities, and the offering of fervent supplications to Almighty God . . . .'

"It is fit and becoming in all people, at all times, to acknowledge and revere the supreme government of God; to bow in humble submission to his chastisements; to confess and deplore their sins and transgressions, in the full conviction that the fear of the Lord is the beginning of wisdom; and to pray with all fervency and contrition for the pardon of their past offenses . . .

"Whereas when our own beloved country, once, by the blessing of God, united, prosperous, and happy, is now afflicted with faction and civil war, it is peculiarly fit for us to recognize the hand of God in this terrible visitation, and in sorrowful remembrance of our own faults and crimes as a

nation and as individuals, to humble ourselves before him and to pray for his mercy.
. . .

"Therefore, I, Abraham Lincoln, President of the United States, do appoint the last Thursday in September next as a day of humiliation, prayer, and fasting for all the people of the nation."

Proclamation of a National Fast Day
March 30, 1863

"Whereas, the Senate of the United States, devoutly recognizing the supreme authority and just government of Almighty God in all the affairs of men and of nations, has by a resolution requested the President to designate and set apart a day for national prayer and humiliation:

"And whereas, it is the duty of nations as well as of men to own their dependence upon the overruling power of God; to confess their sins and transgressions in humble sorrow, yet with assured hope that genuine repentance will lead to mercy and pardon; and to recognize the sublime truth, announced in the Holy Scriptures and proven by all history, that those nations only are blessed whose God is the Lord;

"And insomuch as we know that by his divine law nations, like individuals, are subjected to punishments and chastisements in this world, may we not justly fear that the awful calamity of civil war which now desolates the land may be but a punishment inflicted upon us for our presumptuous sins. . . . We have been the recipients of the choicest bounties of Heaven. We have been preserved, these many years, in peace and prosperity. We have grown in numbers, wealth, and power as no other nation has ever grown; but we have forgotten God. . . . We have vainly imagined, in the deceitfulness of our hearts, that all these blessings were produced by some superior wisdom and virtue of our own. Intoxicated with unbroken success, we have become too self-sufficient to feel the necessity of redeeming and preserving grace, too proud to pray to the God that made us.

"It behooves us, then, to humble ourselves before the offended Power, to confess our national sins, and to pray for clemency and forgiveness. . . .

"I do hereby request all the people to abstain on that day from their ordinary secular pursuits, and to unite at their several places of public worship and their respective homes in keeping the day holy to the Lord. . . . All this being done in sincerity and truth, let us then rest humbly in the hope authorized by the divine teachings, that the united cry of the nation will be heard on high, and answered with blessings no less than the pardon of our national sins, and the restoration of our now divided and suffering country to its former happy condition of unity and peace."

Proclamation for a Day of Prayer
July 7, 1864

"Whereas the Senate and House of Representatives, at their last session, adopted a concurrent resolution, which was approved on the second day of July instant, and which was in the words following, namely:

"That the President of the United States be requested to appoint a day for humiliation and prayer by the people of the United States; that he request his constitutional advisers at the head of the executive departments to unite with him as chief magistrate of the nation, at the city of Washington, and the members of Congress, and all magistrates, all civil, military, and naval officers, all soldiers, sailors, and marines, with all loyal and law-abiding people, to convene at their usual places of worship, or wherever they may be, to confess and to repent of their manifold sins; to implore the compassion and forgiveness of the Almighty . . . to implore him, as the supreme ruler of the world, not to destroy us as a people, nor suffer us to be destroyed by the hostility or the connivance of other nations, or by obstinate adhesion to our own counsels which may be in conflict with his eternal purposes.
. . .

"Now, therefore, I, Abraham Lincoln . . . do hereby appoint the first Thursday of August next to be observed by the people of the United States as a day of national humiliation and prayer.

"I do hereby further invite and request the heads of the executive departments of this government, together with all legislators, all judges and magistrates, and all other persons exercising authority in the land, whether civil, military, or naval, and all soldiers, seamen, and marines in the national service, and all the other loyal and law-abiding people of the United States, to assemble in their preferred places of public worship on that day, and there and then to render to the Almighty and merciful Ruler of the universe such homages and such confessions, and to offer to him such supplications, as the Congress of the United States have, in their aforesaid resolution, so solemnly, so earnestly, and so reverently recommended."

PRAY FOR YOUR LEADERS

1 TIMOTHY 2:1-4,8 • ¹"I urge, then, first of all, that requests, prayers, intercession and thanksgiving be made for everyone— ²for kings and all those in authority, that we may live peaceful and quiet lives in all godliness and holiness. ³This is good, and pleases God our Savior, ⁴who wants all men to be saved and to come to a knowledge of the truth. . . . ⁸I want men everywhere to lift up holy hands in prayer, without anger or disputing.

Are you willing to change your life-style significantly enough to be the kind of person in prayer that God could use to change your church, your city, and our nation? If so:

- Pray that God will display His holiness and bring glory to Himself in His dealings with our nation.
- Pray that God will do whatever is necessary to bring our nation and its leaders to recognize His punishments for their national and individual sins.
- Pray that the leaders will humble themselves before God.
- Pray that our leaders will acknowledge that God is the Sovereign Ruler of men and nations.
- Pray that our leaders will place their dependence on God for direction and trust Him for their help.
- Pray that our leaders will recognize the discipline and judgment of God and call the nation to repent and return to the Lord as their God.
- Pray that the people of our nation will also recognize the discipline and judgment of God and follow our leaders back to God.
- Give God glory, thanksgiving, and praise when He accomplishes His purposes in our nation.

© LifeWay Press, 1993. Used by permission.
* You have permission to reproduce this article from *Fresh Encounter Leader's Manual* for distribution in your church or group.

Biblical quotations are taken from the Holy Bible, *New International Version*, copyright © 1973, 1978, 1984 by International Bible Society.

NOTES

Introductory Session

Ideally the pastor or other primary leader of your church or group should guide this session. The introductory session introduces the study of *God's Pattern for Revival and Spiritual Awakening* to a large group. This large group should include all prospective members for the small-group study. Because of the importance for your church to respond corporately (as a group), this session needs to be conducted at a time when a maximum attendance is possible. Ask God to guide you in deciding the time and place. During the six sessions that follow this introduction, members will meet in small groups.

BEFORE THE SESSION

❑ 1. Secure copies of *God's Pattern for Revival and Spiritual Awakening* for each member you anticipate.
❑ 2. Study the introductory pages 5–12 (GP) and Unit 1.
❑ 3. Prepare a poster of the diagram of God's pattern for revival and spiritual awakening inside the back cover of the member's book. You may want to prepare a simplified drawing like the one below.

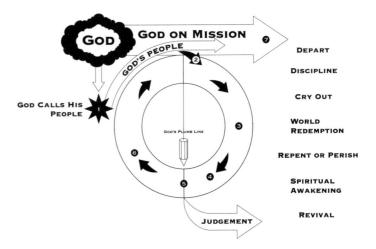

Draw the diagram and include the numbers 1–7. Leave off the key words. On separate pieces of paper or poster board, write the key words for each of the seven phases. Attach Velcro or reusable adhesive so the key words can be placed on the poster and removed. During the study you will be adding and removing the key words as you review God's pattern. You may want to laminate the poster for durability and future use.

❑ 4. Write the following Arrival Activity on a poster, overhead transparency, or chalkboard. If you prefer, prepare copies for each person you anticipate in attendance. You may photocopy LM page 69 to distribute.

> **ARRIVAL ACTIVITY**
>
> In your opinion, what is the spiritual health or condition of the following people and groups? Select one of the lettered items below and write the letter in the blank or write your own statement.
>
> ____ 1. Our nation? ____ 4. Our church?
> ____ 2. Our city/town/community? ____ 5. My family?
> ____ 3. Our denomination? ____ 6. My life?
>
> a. On fire for the Lord!
> b. Going and growing!
> c.. A little under the weather.
> d. Lukewarm, apathetic, indifferent.
> e. Morally, spiritually bankrupt.
> f. Dry as a desert.
> g. Dead or dying.
> h. A fountain of living water.
> i. On the road to recovery.
> j. Cold as ice.
> k. Heading for destruction.
> l. Other: _____

❏ 5. Prepare your own testimony for the "Arrival Activity" above.

❏ 6. Draw a poster of the "Leaning Tower of Pisa" illustrated on LM page 71 or make an overhead transparency for use in a large group.

❏ 7. Secure a videotape player and monitor(s) for showing *An Introduction to Fresh Encounter*. Experts recommend a 21-inch or larger monitor for each 25 persons. A large-screen television or video projection system may be needed for larger groups.

❏ 8. Preview the video *An Introduction to Fresh Encounter*.

❏ 9. Prepare a presentation of the information that the groups are to share in "Content Review" (LM p. 67), number 4.

❏ 10. Be prepared to give the details about the small-group study sessions—who, what, when, where, how long, and so forth.

DURING THE SESSION

ARRIVAL ACTIVITY

1. **Opinion Question.** As members arrive, distribute the "Arrival Activity" worksheets. Ask them to complete the opinion question on the worksheet.

2. **Prayer.** Lead the group in prayer asking the Holy Spirit to work during the session to accomplish all that God has intended for this time.

3. **Read Psalm 96:1-4.** Emphasize the importance of Christians sharing with one another the wonderful deeds God has done.

4. **Testimonies.** Divide into groups of about six each. Ask volunteers in each group to share with the group their most meaningful or moving encounter with God. This could be a personal, family, or church experience. Begin by sharing an example from your life.

5. **Spiritual Health Opinions.** In the same groupings, ask

members to share their responses to the "Arrival Activity" question.

Ask that all members share their opinions on the spiritual health of the nation, then your city or town, then your church, family, and self. Ask the groups to close the sharing time with a brief prayer for God to work in reviving spiritual health where it is needed.

6. **Distribute Books.** Distribute copies of *God's Pattern for Revival and Spiritual Awakening*. Encourage members to write their names on the front covers so they can keep track of their own books. If members are purchasing their own books, receive the money in an appropriate and efficient way. This might take place before or after the session. Or members may place the amount in an offering envelope. Collect funds in a way that will not embarrass anyone who is not able or prepared to contribute.

7. **Audiotapes.** Tell members that there is a series of audiotapes that support *Fresh Encounter*. The 12 messages are for individual use. The first six parallel the six sessions of *God's Pattern for Revival and Spiritual Awakening*. The second six are audio versions of *A Plumb Line for God's People*. Encourage members who use the tapes to share during sessions what they learn.

CONTENT REVIEW

1. **Is God at Work?** Ask for a show of hands in response to the question: "How many of you sense a hunger or need for a fresh encounter with God?" If people sense that need, quote these verses:
   - Romans 3:11—"There is no one who understands, no one who seeks God."
   - John 6:44—"No one can come to me unless the Father who sent me draws him."
   - Philippians 2:13—"It is God who works in you to will and to act according to his good purpose."

   Explain that no one seeks an encounter with God unless God is at work causing the person to seek Him. The fact that God has created that desire for a fresh encounter with Him is an indication that He is at work. God will be at work to complete what He has begun. Indicate that when God gives a hunger corporately, He will fulfill it (see Phil. 1:6).

2. **Introduction to *Fresh Encounter*.** Show the video *An Introduction to Fresh Encounter*. Call attention to the diagram and statement of the seven phases in God's pattern on the worksheets they have been given and on the back flap of the member's book.

3. **Leaning Tower of Pisa.** Call attention to your illustration of the Leaning Tower of Pisa. Relate the illustration of the tower (GP p. 9 or PL p. 6) to the spiritual application. Point out that the leaning tower is a visible symptom of the root problem in the foundation. Spiritually our lack of obedience, the presence of substitutes for God, and other needs resulting from sin are symptoms of a deeper problem—our

love relationship with God isn't right. Point out that God will use this study to help focus attention on our love relationship with Him. The invitation people will face in this process is God's call: "Return to me" (Mal. 3:7).

4. **Invitation to *Fresh Encounter*.** If time permits you may want to lead the small-group activity described below. If you have used the video introduction, you may need to prepare a presentation on these topics to save time.

   Divide into seven or more groups, depending on the number of people present. Do not assign more than eight people to a group. Assign the seven subtopics on GP pages 8–10, one to each group. (You may have more than one group studying each subtopic.) Ask groups to read their subtopic and decide as a group what the key ideas or statements are. Ask each group to select one person to present to the large group a summary of the key ideas in each subtopic. Call on each group for a report on these topics:
   1. God Is at Work
   2. God's Ideal: A Love Relationship
   3. Sin Brings Discipline
   4. God's Invitation: Return to Your First Love
   5. God's Plumb Line
   6. Revival
   7. Spiritual Awakening

GOD'S PATTERN
1. **Overview God's Pattern.** (Provide this overview only if you did not use the video introduction.) Display the poster you have prepared. Ask members to turn to the inside back cover of their books to see God's pattern for revival and spiritual awakening. Ask a member to read the seven phases, one at a time. As each phase is read, place the key word(s) on your poster and briefly explain each phase.
2. **Warning.** Summarize the warning given on GP page 11. Emphasize how serious obedience will be and that any study of God's Word is an immediate encounter with God (see Matt. 18:19-20; Rev. 1-3).
3. **Study Tips.** Using the study tips on GP page 12, give the members an overview of the study. Point out sample pages in the member's book where appropriate:
   - Unit page—page 13
   - Memorize Scripture—back of the book
   - Revival accounts—page 14
   - "Cleansing by Washing with Water Through the Word"—page 15
   - Daily lesson—pages 16–17
   - "Encountering God in Prayer"—page 17
   - Unit review—page 26
4. **Group Study.** Explain the small-group study plan you have developed. Discuss time, starting date, place, groupings, leadership, cost, and so forth. Remind members that they need to complete the five lessons in Unit 1 prior to the first session of the study.

NOTES

5. **Questions.** Answer any questions people may have about the study.

PRAYER TRIPLETS

Closing Prayer. Divide into prayer triplets (groups of three). Ask triplets to pray for the upcoming study, for each other, for their pastor, for other church and denominational leaders, and for revival to come to your city and the nation. You may want to distribute copies of "Pray for Revival in the Land" (LM p. 61) for use in the coming weeks and months.

AFTER THE SESSION

1. Secure additional copies of *God's Pattern for Revival and Spiritual Awakening* if needed.
2. Determine whether you have enough small-group leaders for the number of groups you will need. If you do not, enlist and orient additional leaders.
3. Invite people to the study one more time to get maximum participation by next week's session.
4. Make sure provision has been made for newcomers after the first or second session.
5. If you have not already done so, prepare the worksheets needed for the following sessions.
6. Save the "God's Pattern" poster for later use.

Introducing God's Pattern for Revival and Spiritual Awakening

In your opinion, what is the spiritual health or condition of the following people or groups? Select one of the lettered items at the right and write the letter in the blank, or write your own statement.

_____ 1. Our nation

_____ 2. Our city/town/community

_____ 3. Our denomination

_____ 4. Our church

_____ 5. My family

_____ 6. My life

a. On fire for the Lord
b. Going and growing
c. A little under the weather
d. Lukewarm, apathetic, indifferent
e. Morally, spiritually bankrupt
f. Dry as a desert
g. Dead or dying
h. A fountain of living water
i. On the road to recovery
j. Cold as ice
k. Heading for destruction
l. Other: _____

PHASE 1: God is on mission to redeem a lost world. God calls His people into a relationship with Himself, and He accomplishes His work through them.

PHASE 2: God's people tend to depart from Him, turning to substitutes for His presence, purposes, and ways.

PHASE 3: God disciplines His people out of His love for them.

PHASE 4: God's people cry out to Him for help.

PHASE 5: God calls His people to repent and return to Him or perish.

PHASE 6: God revives His repentant people by restoring them to a right relationship with Himself.

PHASE 7: God exalts His Son Jesus in His people and draws the lost to saving faith in Him.

© LifeWay Press, 1993. Used by Permission.
* You have permission to reproduce this worksheet from *Fresh Encounter Leader's Manual* for use in the introductory session of your study of *God's Pattern for Revival and Spiritual Awakening*.

Seven Phases In God's Pattern

PHASE 1: GOD IS ON MISSION TO REDEEM A LOST WORLD. HE CALLS A PEOPLE INTO A RELATIONSHIP WITH HIMSELF, AND HE ACCOMPLISHES HIS WORK THROUGH THEM.

PHASE 2: GOD'S PEOPLE TEND TO DEPART FROM HIM TURNING TO SUBSTITUTES FOR HIS PRESENCE, HIS PURPOSES, AND HIS WAYS.

PHASE 3: GOD DISCIPLINES HIS PEOPLE BECAUSE OF HIS LOVE.

PHASE 4: GOD'S PEOPLE CRY OUT TO HIM FOR HELP.

PHASE 5: GOD CALLS HIS PEOPLE TO REPENT AND RETURN TO HIM OR PERISH.

PHASE 6: GOD REVIVES HIS REPENTANT PEOPLE BY RESTORING THEM TO A RIGHT RELATIONSHIP WITH HIMSELF.

PHASE 7: GOD EXALTS HIS SON JESUS IN HIS PEOPLE AND DRAWS THE LOST TO SAVING FAITH IN HIM.

© Lifeway Press 1993. Used by permission.
* You have permission to make an overhead cel from this sheet in *Fresh Encounter Leader's Manual* for use in your study of *God's Pattern for Revival and Spiritual Awakening*.

Leaning Tower of Pisa

© Lifeway Press 1993. Used by permission.
* You have permission to make an overhead cel from this sheet in *Fresh Encounter Leader's Manual* for use in your study of *God's Pattern for Revival and Spiritual Awakening*.

NOTES

Session 1:
An Overview of God's Pattern

BEFORE THE SESSION

Remember: The following plans are suggestions. Let God Himself be your guide in all things and at all times (read again 2 Cor. 9:8).

❏ 1. Study Unit 1 of *God's Pattern for Revival and Spiritual Awakening* and complete the learning activities.
❏ 2. Pray for your group members during the week. Ask God to guide you as you prepare for this session. Ask God to prepare the hearts of His people for a fresh encounter with Him.
❏ 3. Read "During the Session" and allow the Holy Spirit to guide you as to which activities to use and how much time to devote to each. You may not have time to deal with all of these activities in one session. Don't let that frustrate you. God will guide you in deciding which activities will be most helpful to your group. You may need to schedule a second or third meeting for God to work in the hearts of His people.
❏ 4. If you have not already done so, prepare a poster of God's pattern for revival and spiritual awakening. Refer to instructions on LM page 64.
❏ 5. Prayer triplets may want to get all three persons on the telephone at the same time to pray together during the week. Contact your local phone company and secure instructions on how to make a conference call (more than two parties connected at the same time). Find out how much the call costs. Be prepared to share instructions with the group.
❏ 6. Provide six pieces of poster board or newsprint and markers for use during the arrival activity. Also provide masking tape for mounting the paper or posters on the wall. Place supplies on tables (if available) or on the floor in the center of the room. List the four subjects about the early church on a poster board or chalkboard (see Arrival Activity, number 2).
❏ 7. If you plan to use the worksheet "A Revival Under Samuel" (LM p. 77), make one copy for each group member.
❏ 8. Provide copies of *God's Pattern for Revival and Spiritual Awakening* for persons who may be joining the group for the first time.
❏ 9. Arrange chairs in a semicircle facing a focal wall. Display the "God's Pattern" poster on the wall.

DURING THE SESSION

Arrival Activity

1. **Greet members as they arrive.** Assign each member a chapter number from Acts 1–6. After you have assigned each of the six chapter numbers to six different people, start over again. Members with the same chapter number should begin working together on the following assignment. If you plan to use the optional study of revival under Samuel, create a seventh group to study the worksheet.

2. **The Early Church.** Ask members to read through their assigned chapter in Acts and look for the four subjects listed below. Ask members to record their findings on the newsprint or poster board provided.
   a. Supernatural things God did.
   b. Activities of the believers and apostles that contributed to spiritual vitality.
   c. Relationships between believers.
   d. Positive responses of the world to God and His church.

3. **Optional: A Revival Under Samuel.** Distribute copies of the worksheet on LM page 77 to the seventh group. While the others work on number 2 above, ask this group to complete the worksheet and summarize the revival for the rest of the members.

4. **Opening Prayer.** Lead in an opening prayer. Ask the Holy Spirit to reveal the nature of a church that pleases God and that can be used in spiritual awakening.

5. **Early Church Reports.** Ask for one person from each chapter-group to report their findings on the supernatural things God did. Get reports from all six groups. Then follow the same process for the other three topics. Conclude by pointing out that this is probably the purest example in Scripture of what a church was created to be.

   Ask: What do you see as the major similarities and differences between the early church in Acts and our church in our—
   - demonstration of God's supernatural power?
   - activities?
   - relationships between believers?
   - positive responses of the world?

God's Pattern

1. **Review Phases.** Display the "God's Pattern" poster. Ask volunteers to help you match the key words with the appropriate phase number on the poster. Mix up the key words. Then call them out one at a time and ask with which phase the key word goes. Place it on the poster and call out the next word. Continue until members have helped you correctly place the key words on the poster.

2. **Revival Under Samuel Report.** If you created a seventh group to study the revival under Samuel, ask them to summarize the revival. Ask them to identify the similarities in this revival and in God's pattern for revival and spiritual awakening.

CONTENT REVIEW

1. **Scripture Memory Verse.** Ask for a volunteer to quote 2 Chronicles 7:14 and identify the four requirements for revival.
2. **Revival.** Ask a volunteer to define revival and give an example from the Bible of a revival that took place among God's people (for example, revival under Ezra and Nehemiah).
3. **Spiritual Awakening.** Ask a volunteer to define spiritual awakening and give an example from the Bible of a spiritual awakening that took place among God's people (for example, awakening on the Day of Pentecost).

ENCOUNTERING GOD

1. **Most Meaningful.** Ask members to turn to the unit review on GP page 26. Ask volunteers to share the statement, Scripture, or idea that was most meaningful to them. Encourage those who will to share their prayer response to God.
2. **What Is the Spirit Saying?** Ask: As you studied and prayed this week, what has God been saying to you about your life, your family, or our church?

DISCUSSION QUESTIONS

As time permits, guide members to discuss the following questions.

1. Review the cycle of sin and revival on GP page 20. Ask: Where do you sense our nation is in this cycle of sin and revival? Why?
2. Read Judges 2:14 and ask: Who are some of the "raiders" God may use in our day to discipline His people?
3. Point to the poster "God's Pattern." Ask: Where do you sense our church is in God's pattern for revival and spiritual awakening? Why?
4. Ask members to turn to GP page 24. Ask: What is the most unusual fact you read in the revival under Ezra and Nehemiah? Why do you sense that is so unusual?
5. Why is worship an important element in revival?
6. Why do you think it was important for Nehemiah to rehearse the mighty acts of God during this revival meeting? How meaningful would it be for our church to remember all the ways God has worked in our church in years past?

SPIRITUAL AWAKENING IN WALES (GP P. 14)

Ask: Why was each of these factors important in the awakening in Wales in 1904–5?

1. The sense of need by the people.
2. The work of God in preparing the principality for revival.
3. The prayer meetings before the revival began.
4. The burdened heart of Evan Roberts.
5. The brokenness and cleansing of God's people.
6. The four points of Evan's message.

CLEANSING BY WASHING WITH WATER THROUGH THE WORD

Ask members to turn to "Cleansing by Washing with Water Through the Word" on GP page 15.

1. **Wash Out.** Ask members to identify the things they marked that would be important to "wash out" of a person's life.
2. **Wash In.** Ask members to identify the things they marked that would be valuable to "wash in" to a person's life.
3. **Responding to God.** Ask: What, if anything, has God said to you through these Scriptures and how are you responding to Him?

PRAYER TRIPLETS

Divide members into groups of three. Try to keep the same groupings throughout the study. Ask prayer triplets to pray together about the following concerns:

1. **Petition for One Another.** Encourage members to share specific concerns related to self or family for which the others can pray. Ask members to place an emphasis on spiritual concerns rather than physical concerns.
2. **Intercession for Our Church.** Ask triplets to pray that your church would become the kind of church God could use to bring spiritual awakening to your town or city.
3. **Continue Praying.** Encourage prayer triplets to continue praying for each other during the coming week. Suggest they may want to get together during the week to pray. If they cannot meet together they may want to call each other to pray. Give instructions on how to make a conference call if triplets should desire to do so.

AFTER THE SESSION

1. Make notes to yourself about your group members and ways you sense a need to pray for each of them. Pray specifically for one or two group members each day during the week. This week pray that "Cleansing by Washing with Water Through the Word" will help each member come to a clear understanding about their relationship to Christ.
2. Ask yourself the following questions and jot notes in the margin or on a separate sheet of paper.
   - What major differences did my group find between our church and the church in Acts? What, if anything, did members mention that they would like to see changed to be more like the church in Acts?
   - What idea or information surfaced that may indicate conviction of sin?
   - Do I have any real prayer warriors in my group that might want to get together to pray at a different time during the week? (List their names and consider encouraging their participation in a special prayer time. Discuss this during your leadership team meeting this week.)
   - What spiritual or mental preparation do I need to make for the next session that may have been lacking this week?

NOTES

NOTES

- Which of the members need to be encouraged to participate more in the sharing and discussion times? When and how will I encourage them?
- When could I have responded more appropriately to the needs of members or to the leadership of the Holy Spirit?

3. If your group had more than ten members, consider dividing it into smaller groups. Work with the Fresh Encounter facilitator to make arrangements this week.
4. Read "Before the Session" in the next session to get an idea of the preparation that will be required for your next group session.
5. Attend your leadership team meeting this week. Write down any concerns you may want to discuss during that meeting.

A Revival Under Samuel

Following the cycle we see in the Book of Judges, the Israelites had departed from the Lord. They went to battle against the Philistines during the days of Eli the priest. In the battle they lost 4,000 men. The leaders returned to camp and asked, "Why did the Lord bring defeat upon us today before the Philistines? Let us bring the ark of the Lord's covenant from Shiloh, so that it may go with us and save us from the hand of our enemies" (1 Sam. 4:3).

1. Where did the leaders of Israel's army get their directions? Check one.

❏ a. They sought their directions from God, and God told them what to do.
❏ b. They discussed the problem and used their own reasoning to decide what to do.

2. The leaders decided to place their trust in . . . (check one)

❏ a. God
❏ b. The ark of the covenant

A Substitute for God

The Israelites made a serious mistake. They thought they could take the initiative and control God's actions in their behalf. They did not seek directions from the Lord. They used their own reasoning (1b).

Then they substituted the ark of the covenant (2b) for God. The ark was to represent God's presence among His people. However, they made a subtle but significant shift in their thinking. They shifted their trust from God Almighty to the ark itself. They took "it" with them so "it" would save them.

God's Discipline

"It" did not save them, and they lost 30,000 soldiers in the battle that day. The ark was captured and Eli's two sons were killed. Upon hearing the news, Eli fell over, broke his neck, and died.

The Philistines returned the ark to Israel seven months later, and it was taken to Kiriath Jearim for safe keeping. During the time that followed, Israel was without the manifest presence of God.

1 Samuel 7:2-4

²It was a long time, twenty years in all, that the ark remained at Kiriath Jearim, and all the people of Israel mourned and sought after the Lord. ³And Samuel said to the whole house of Israel, "If you are returning to the Lord with all your hearts, then rid yourselves of the foreign gods and the Ashtoreths and commit yourselves to the Lord and serve him only, and he will deliver you out of the hand of the Philistines." ⁴So the Israelites put away their Baals and Ashtoreths, and served the Lord only.

3. In 1 Samuel 7:2, how did the people respond after 20 years of discipline?

_____

4. Complete the following for 1 Samuel 7:3-4.

a. Circle the words that indicate they were to return to a love relationship with God.
b. Underline the things they were to get rid of or turn away from.

Repentance and Revival/Restoration

Twenty years later, the people cried out to God. They "mourned and sought after the Lord." Samuel led them to repent by getting rid of their foreign gods and returning to the Lord.

5. Read 1 Samuel 7:5-9 and circle the words that describe what Israel and Samuel did.

1 Samuel 7:5-9

⁵Then Samuel said, "Assemble all Israel at Mizpah and I will intercede with the Lord for you." ⁶When they had assembled at Mizpah, they drew water and poured it out before the Lord. On that day they fasted and there they confessed, "We have sinned against the Lord." And Samuel was leader of Israel at Mizpah.

⁷When the Philistines heard that Israel had assembled at Mizpah, the rulers of the Philistines came up to attack them. And when the Israelites heard of it, they were afraid because of the Philistines. ⁸They said to Samuel, "Do not stop crying out to the Lord our God for us, that he may rescue us from the hand of the Philistines." ⁹Then Samuel took a suckling lamb and offered it up as a whole burnt offering to the Lord. He cried out to the Lord on Israel's behalf, and the Lord answered him.

Israel met together as a group to fast, confess their sin, and offer sacrifices of water and a lamb. Samuel, as a spiritual leader, prayed for the people and God answered him.

1 SAMUEL 7:10-13

¹⁰While Samuel was sacrificing the burnt offering, the Philistines drew near to engage Israel in battle. But that day the Lord thundered with loud thunder against the Philistines and threw them into such a panic that they were routed before the Israelites.

¹²Then Samuel took a stone and set it up between Mizpah and Shen. He named it Ebenezer, saying, "Thus far has the Lord helped us." [Ebenezer means "stone of help."] ¹³So the Philistines were subdued and did not invade Israelite territory again.

Throughout Samuel's lifetime, the hand of the Lord was against the Philistines.

6. How long did God keep the Philistines subdued?

_____
_____

SUMMARY

Do you see how God related to His people? When they departed from Him, God disciplined them. When they cried out to Him and repented of their wickedness, God heard their cry, delivered them from their enemy, and restored them to a right relationship with Himself.

© LifeWay Press, 1993. Used by permission.
* You have permission to reproduce this worksheet from *Fresh Encounter Leader's Manual* for use in session 1 of your study of *God's Pattern for Revival and Spiritual Awakening*.

Biblical quotations are taken from the Holy Bible, *New International Version*, copyright © 1973, 1978, 1984 by International Bible Society.

Session 2: God Is on Mission in Our World

BEFORE THE SESSION

❏ 1. Study Unit 2 of *God's Pattern for Revival and Spiritual Awakening* and complete the learning activities.
❏ 2. Pray for your group members during the week. Ask God to guide you as you prepare for this session. Ask God to prepare the hearts of His people for a fresh encounter with Him.
❏ 3. Read "During the Session" and allow the Holy Spirit to guide you as to which of the activities to use and how much time to devote to each. You may not have time to deal with all of these activities in one session.
❏ 4. Duplicate the "God at Work" worksheets on LM page 84. Provide a copy for subgroups of three people. If you prefer, copy the information on a poster board or newsprint.

GOD AT WORK

God is already at work in His world. God has called your church to join Him in the work He is doing. In groups of three, discuss the following questions:

1. Where are some of the places God is at work through your church? Mark them with an "A." Think of people God is using in these places.
2. Where are some places you sense God wants to work through your church? Mark them with a "B." Mark only those places that your group senses God may want to touch through your church.

__ countries of the world   __ remote tribes
__ high school campuses   __ inner cities
__ military units   __ hospitals
__ prisons   __ nursing homes
__ apartment complexes   __ rural communities
__ office building   __ hurting people
__ homeless   __ homebound
__ poor people   __ board rooms
__ college/university   __ factory lines
    campuses   __ government: city,
                                  state, national
__ others_____

❏ 5. Cut out LM pages 85–86 and either laminate them or cover them with clear adhesive shelf paper. If you prefer

NOTES

NOTES

larger versions: on separate sheets of paper or poster board, draw enlarged versions of the "Love Relationship" diagram on LM page 85 and the "Redemption" diagram on LM page 86.
❏ 6. Prepare a poster expressing the love of Christ for us. Find a picture or several pictures of the crucifixion or use the one below. You may be able to borrow one from a children's teacher at your church. Place the picture on a piece of poster board and write the following text above or below the picture: "Having loved his own . . . he now showed them the full extent of His love" (John 13:1, NIV). Display the poster during the session.

❏ 7. Provide copies of *God's Pattern for Revival and Spiritual Awakening* for persons who may be joining the group for the first time. This should be the last week you accept new members. Check what arrangements have been made by your church for people who want to become involved in the study after the second session.
❏ 8. Arrange the chairs in a semicircle facing a focal wall. Display the "God's Pattern" poster on the wall.

DURING THE SESSION

ARRIVAL ACTIVITY
1. **Greet members as they arrive.** Call attention to the "God at Work" poster or distribute the worksheets you have prepared. Ask members to complete the worksheets in groups of three.
2. **Opening Prayer.** Call on a member to open your session with prayer.
3. **Reports.** Ask groups to report on their discussion during the "God at Work" activity.

GOD'S PATTERN
Focus Phase of the Week. Display the key words for the seven phases on the wall beside the poster or lay them on a table or on the floor in front of the poster. Ask a volunteer to select the key word for phase 1, place it on the poster, and state phase 1 in his own words.

CONTENT REVIEW
1. **Scripture Memory Verse.** Ask for a volunteer to quote 1 Peter 2:9. Ask: What are the four ways God describes His people, and what does each mean for a church?

2. **Creation and a Love Relationship.** Ask a volunteer to use the "Love Relationship" diagram (LM p. 85 and explain in his own words God's original intention for the people He created.
3. **Redemption.** Ask a different volunteer to use the "Redemption" diagram (LM p. 86) and explain in her own words what God has done to provide our redemption.
4. **God's People.** Ask a volunteer to explain how Abraham and Israel were involved in God's plan for calling out a people for God's purposes.
5. **Fellow Workers.** Ask a volunteer to use the "God's Pattern" poster and describe how God's people become involved in His mission.

ENCOUNTERING GOD
1. **Most Meaningful.** Ask members to turn to the unit review on GP page 40. Call on volunteers to share the statement, Scripture, or idea that was most meaningful to them. Encourage those who will to share their prayer response to God.
2. **What Is the Spirit Saying?** Ask: As you studied and prayed this week, what has God been saying to you about your life, your family, or our church?

DISCUSSION QUESTIONS
As time permits, guide members to discuss the following questions.
1. What does *redemption* mean?
2. What does *reconciliation* mean?
3. What does *dead in sin* mean?
4. What makes the people of God special? What percentage of the members of our church do you think are living in the joy, wonder, and awe of being God's chosen and treasured possessions?
5. What does a church do to function as a royal priesthood? How faithfully is our church practicing our priesthood before God?
6. How faithfully are we declaring God's praises to a world in darkness? Are we shining brightly as the "light of the world"?
7. What are we doing as a church body to represent one another's spiritual needs to God?
8. How separate are we from the world and its ways? What evidences can we give that we are holy and set apart for God's service?
9. Do we act as a church as if we can do nothing apart from God? Why do you think we do or do not?

THE SHANTUNG REVIVAL (GP P. 28)
1. **Response.** Ask the following questions:
   - What was your primary response to the report on the Shantung Revival?
   - Did God use it to encourage, instruct, inspire, challenge, or convict you? How?

2. **Application.** Discuss one or more of the following questions:
   - How can a church help people make sure they have been converted before they join the church?
   - Why is it important for a church to have a redeemed church membership?

Cleansing by Washing with Water Through the Word

Ask members to turn to "Cleansing by Washing with Water Through the Word" on GP page 29.

1. **Evidence.** Ask members: What are some of the evidences that a person has experienced a new birth of the Spirit? What are some things that might cause a person to seriously question whether he or she has experienced the new birth?
2. **Responding to God.** Ask: What, if anything, has God said to you through these Scriptures and how are you responding to Him?

Prayer Triplets

Ask prayer triplets to pray together about the following concerns:

1. **Petition for One Another.** Ask triplets to pray for each other with a focus on spiritual vitality. Suggest they use Paul's prayer for the church at Ephesus as a model:

   > [16] "I pray that out of his glorious riches he may strengthen you with power through his Spirit in your inner being, [17] so that Christ may dwell in your hearts through faith. And I pray that you, being rooted and established in love, [18] may have power, together with all the saints, to grasp how wide and long and high and deep is the love of Christ, [19] and to know this love that surpasses knowledge—that you may be filled to the measure of all the fullness of God."
   >
   > –Ephesians 3:16-19

2. **Praise and Thanksgiving.** Call attention to the poster on the love of Christ. Ask triplets to take time to express praise, adoration, and thanksgiving to God for loving, choosing, saving, forgiving, and calling us to be a part of His mission to redeem the world.
3. **Continue Praying.** Encourage prayer triplets to continue praying for each other during the coming week. Suggest they get together during the week to pray.

AFTER THE SESSION

1. Make notes to yourself about your group members and ways you sense a need to pray for each of them. This week pray that the Holy Spirit will reveal to members any ways they or your church may have departed from God.
2. Ask yourself the following questions and jot notes in the margin or on a separate sheet of paper.

- What are the major areas members sensed God is at work in and around our church?
- Which (if any) of my members struggled with the activity regarding the evidence for their salvation? Do I need to call or visit any of these? If so, when will I do it?
- What subject areas seemed confusing or unfamiliar to members? Does our pastor need to do some extra preaching or teaching on any of these subjects? (Plan to share these during the leadership team meeting.)
- In which (if any) areas did members believe our church falls short of God's design for His people?
- What spiritual or mental preparation do I need to make for the next session that may have been lacking this week?
- Which of the members need to be encouraged to participate more in the sharing and discussion times? When and how will I encourage them?
- When could I have responded more appropriately to the needs of members or to the leadership of the Holy Spirit?

3. Read "Before the Session" in the next session to get an idea of the preparation that will be required for your next group session.
4. Attend your leadership team meeting this week. Write down any concerns you may want to discuss during that meeting.

GOD AT WORK

God is already at work in His world. He has called our church to join Him in the work He is doing. In groups of three, discuss the following questions.
1. Where are some of the places God already is working through our church? Mark them with an "A." Think of people God already is using in these places.
2. Where are some places you sense God wants to work through our church? Mark them with a "B." Mark only those that your group senses God may want to touch through our church.

__ other countries of the world
__ inner cities
__ military units
__ prisons
__ apartment complexes
__ office buildings
__ homeless people
__ poor people
__ college/university campuses
__ government: city, state, national

__ remote tribes
__ high school campuses
__ hospitals
__ nursing homes
__ rural communities
__ hurting people
__ homebound people
__ board rooms
__ factory lines
__ others _____

GOD AT WORK

God is already at work in His world. He has called our church to join Him in the work He is doing. In groups of three, discuss the following questions.
1. Where are some of the places God already is working through our church? Mark them with an "A." Think of people God already is using in these places.
2. Where are some places you sense God wants to work through our church? Mark them with a "B." Mark only those that your group senses God may want to touch through our church.

__ other countries of the world
__ inner cities
__ military units
__ prisons
__ apartment complexes
__ office buildings
__ homeless people
__ poor people
__ college/university campuses
__ government: city, state, national

__ remote tribes
__ high school campuses
__ hospitals
__ nursing homes
__ rural communities
__ hurting people
__ homebound people
__ board rooms
__ factory lines
__ others _____

© LifeWay Press, 1993. Used by Permission.
* You have permission to reproduce this worksheet from *Fresh Encounter Leader's Manual* for use in session 2 of your study of *God's Pattern for Revival and Spiritual Awakening*.

Love Relationship

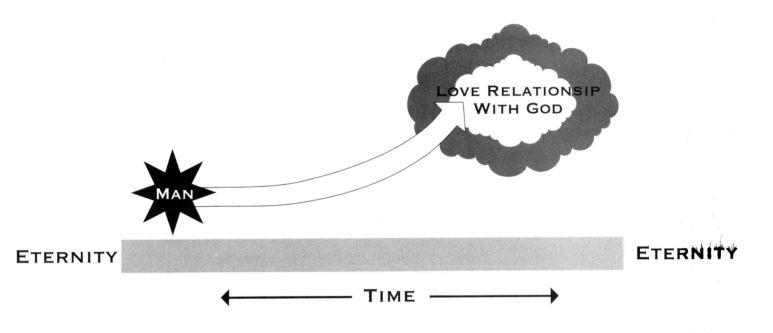

© LifeWay Press, 1993. Used by Permission.
* You have permission to reproduce this worksheet from *Fresh Encounter Leader's Manual* for use in session 2 of your study of *God's Pattern for Revival and Spiritual Awakening*.

Redemption

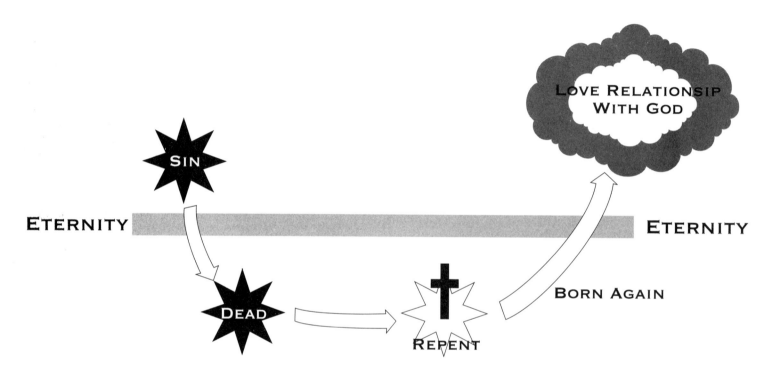

© LifeWay Press, 1993. Used by Permission.
* You have permission to reproduce this worksheet from *Fresh Encounter Leader's Manual* for use in session 2 of your study of *God's Pattern for Revival and Spiritual Awakening*.

Session 3: God's People Tend to Depart

BEFORE THE SESSION

❑ 1. Study Unit 3 of *God's Pattern for Revival and Spiritual Awakening* and complete the learning activities.
❑ 2. Pray for your group members during the week. Ask God to guide you as you prepare for this session. Ask God to prepare the hearts of His people for a fresh encounter with Him.
❑ 3. Read "During the Session" and allow the Holy Spirit to guide you as to which of the activities to use and how much time to devote to each. You may not have time to deal with all of these activities in one session.
❑ 4. Work through the arrival activity. Make your own lists from Isaiah 1 so you will be familiar with the responses to expect.
❑ 5. You will be using the diagrams on LM pages 93–96 in this session. You may want to leave them in this book, or you may want to cut them out and have them laminated for use now and in the future.
❑ 6. Duplicate copies of the "Heart Idols" worksheet on LM page 92 or write the following on a poster board.

HEART IDOLS

Identify each action in the list below as (S) sexual immorality, (I) impurity, or (G) greed.
____ a. Having material possessions but refusing to help a person in need.
____ b. Reading and looking at pornographic or obscene books and magazines.
____ c. Watching television shows and movies that contain vulgarity and sexual situations.
____ d. Having a sexual affair with a person not your spouse.
____ e. Refusing to give a tithe of your income to God and using it on yourself.
____ f. Participating in sexual relationships with family members who are not your spouse.
____ g. Taking unfair advantage of people to make more money for yourself.
____ h. Telling and listening to dirty jokes.

❑ 7. Enlist one of your group members to record responses to discussion question 8 (LM p. 89). Save these responses for sharing with church leadership when requested.
❑ 8. Arrange the chairs in a semicircle facing a focal wall. Display the "God's Pattern" poster on the wall. Leave the key words for phase 1 in place.

NOTES

NOTES

DURING THE SESSION

ARRIVAL ACTIVITY
1. **Greet members as they arrive.** Assign members to one of two groups. Ask Group 1 to begin reading Isaiah 1:1-15 and list (1) the things the people were doing that displeased God and (2) the things God commanded the people to do. Ask Group 2 to make the same lists from Isaiah 1:16-31. Be aware that Group 1 will not find many commands for item 2 in their passage.
2. **Opening Prayer.** Ask each group to begin the session with conversational prayer. As both groups pray, quietly ask the Holy Spirit to use you during the session.
3. **Reports.** Call on each group to report their findings from Isaiah 1. Ask: Are we doing the same things God's people were doing in Judah and Jerusalem?

GOD'S PATTERN
1. **Review Phases.** Call attention to the poster. Point to phase 1 and ask for a volunteer to state the phase in her own words.
2. **Focus Phase of the Week.** Display the key words for phases 2–7 on the wall beside the poster or lay them on a table or the floor in front of the poster. Ask a volunteer to select the key word for phase 2, place it on the poster, and state phase 2 in his own words.

CONTENT REVIEW
1. **Scripture Memory Verse.** Ask for a volunteer to quote Hebrews 3:12-13.
2. **Departure.** Ask members to name three steps we take in departing from God. (Answer: heart shift, failure to obey, turning to idols or substitutes)
3. **Heart Shift.** Ask members to divide into groups of three or four. Ask groups to turn to GP page 47 and discuss their answers to the questions.
4. **Idols of the Heart.** Ask members to name some common idols of the heart (see Eph. 5:3-5; answer: sexual immorality, impurity, greed). Distribute the "Heart Idols" worksheets. Ask members to complete the activity and then discuss their answers in groups of three. (Answers: S–d,f; I–b,c,h; G–a,e,g.) Comment: God is pure, holy, and righteous. All of these actions are opposite to God's character. A person who practices these types of actions has given his heart to something other than God.

    Ask members to identify other actions that would be classified as sexual immorality, impurity, and greed.

    Ask members to turn to GP page 51 and, as a group, check answers. Ask various members to read the Scriptures and identify their answers about the substitute mentioned.
5. **Substitutes.** Ask members to name a possible substitute for each of the following: God, God's presence, God's purposes, and God's ways (see GP pp. 51–53). (For example: God—money or career; presence—methods or programs;

purposes—selfish pleasure rather than meeting needs; ways—walk by sight not by faith.)

ENCOUNTERING GOD

1. **Most Meaningful.** Ask members to turn to the unit review on GP page 54. Call on volunteers to share the statements, Scriptures, or ideas that were most meaningful to them. Encourage those who will to share their prayer responses to God.
2. **What Is the Spirit Saying?** Ask: As you studied and prayed this week, what has God been saying to you about your life, your family, or our church?

HEART IDOLS

1. **Television Family.** Show the picture of the family sitting around a television set (LM p. 93). Say: Suppose this is a typical family. Describe the way they spend their time. Describe their family life. Describe their religious life.
2. **Buddhist.** Show the picture of the Buddhist (LM p. 95). Say: Suppose this is a typical Buddhist. Though you may not know many details, try to describe the way he spends his time. Describe his family life. Describe his religious life.
3. **Compare and Contrast.** Ask:
   - In what ways are these people different in their love relationships with God?
   - In what ways are these people similar in their love relationships with God?
4. **Conclusions.** Show the Buddhist again. Ask: What would this person need to do to move into a right love relationships with God?

   Show the television family again. Ask: What changes do you think God might require of this family for them to return to a faithful love relationship with Him?

DISCUSSION QUESTIONS

As time permits, guide members to discuss the following questions.
1. Why do we often allow our hearts to shift?
2. Do you think we can ever get out of the cycle of sin and repentance? Why or why not?
3. What difference should the presence of the Holy Spirit make in the life of a believer regarding her obedience?
4. How can we learn to identify a heart shift early in the cycle instead of waiting for God's discipline or judgment? What are some of the signs?
5. After reading Jeremiah 2:2-13 (GP p. 48), how do you think God feels when His people choose to forsake Him?
6. What are some ways people today are living life like the woman at the well?
7. How do idols of the heart affect our love relationship with God? What does God expect us to do with idols of the heart and why?
8. Ask members to turn to GP page 53. You may want to take a poll of each item. Ask: What are some ways our church

NOTES

may have turned to substitutes for God, His presence, purposes, or ways? What do you sense we may need to do to change our ways? (Leader: get someone to write down these opinions and save them. At some point, church leaders should study the suggestions and seek God's perspective on each one.)

THE FIRST GREAT AWAKENING (GP P. 42)
Response. Ask:
- What was your primary response to the report on the First Great Awakening? Why?
- Did God use it to encourage, instruct, inspire, challenge, or convict you? How?

CLEANSING BY WASHING WITH WATER THROUGH THE WORD
Ask members to turn to "Cleansing by Washing with Water Through the Word" on GP page 43.
1. **Wash Out.** Ask members to identify the things they marked that would be important to "wash out."
2. **Wash In.** Ask members to identify the things they marked that would be valuable to "wash in."
3. **Responding to God.** Ask: What, if anything, has God said to you through these Scriptures? How are you responding to Him?

PRAYER TRIPLETS
Ask prayer triplets to pray together about the following concerns:
1. **Petition for One Another.** Encourage individuals to share one area where they sense they have turned to substitutes for God, His presence, purposes, or ways. Then ask them to pray for each other in that specific area.
2. **Intercession for Our Church.** Ask triplets to pray that God will guide church staff and leaders to identify every way the church may have turned to substitutes. Ask them to pray that God will prepare church members to make the necessary adjustments to change in those areas.
3. **Continue Praying.** Encourage prayer triplets to continue praying for each other during the coming week. Suggest that they get together during the week to pray.

AFTER THE SESSION

1. Make notes to yourself about your group members and ways you sense a need to pray for each of them. Are any members under great conviction about having departed from God? This week pray that God will help members recognize anything happening in their lives, families, or your church that may be discipline from God.
2. Ask yourself the following questions and jot notes in the margin or on a separate sheet of paper.
   - Are any members resisting the study or mounting

arguments against the truths revealed? Who? What are their concerns?
- Do these arguments fit in any of the categories described in the warning on GP page 11?
- In what ways (if any) did members sense that our church has departed from God or turned to substitutes? (List these for sharing in the leadership team meeting.)
- Did members describe any specific event or decision where they sensed our church has departed? What or when was it?
- What helps do families need in developing better television viewing habits? What can our church do to help?
- What spiritual or mental preparation do I need to make for the next session that may have been lacking this week?
- Which of the members need to be encouraged to participate more in the sharing and discussion times? When and how will I encourage them?
- When could I have responded more appropriately to the needs of members or to the leadership of the Holy Spirit?
3. Read "Before the Session" in the next session to get an idea of the preparation that will be required for your next group session.
4. Attend your leadership team meeting this week. Write down any concerns you may want to discuss during that meeting.

Heart Idols

Identify each action in the list below as (S) sexual immorality, (I) impurity, or (G) greed.

____ a. Having material possessions but refusing to help a person in need.

____ b. Reading and looking at pornographic or obscene books and magazines.

____ c. Watching television shows and movies that contain vulgarity and sexual situations.

____ d. Having a sexual affair with a person not your spouse.

____ e. Refusing to give a tithe of your income to God and using it on yourself.

____ f. Participating in sexual relationships with family members who are not your spouse.

____ g. Taking unfair advantage of people to make more money for yourself.

____ h. Telling and listening to "dirty" jokes.

God is pure, holy, and righteous. All of the actions above are opposite to God's character. A person who practices these types of actions has given his heart to something other than God.

(Answers: S=d,f; I=b,c,h; G=a,e,g.)

Heart Idols

Identify each action in the list below as (S) sexual immorality, (I) impurity, or (G) greed.

____ a. Having material possessions but refusing to help a person in need.

____ b. Reading and looking at pornographic or obscene books and magazines.

____ c. Watching television shows and movies that contain vulgarity and sexual situations.

____ d. Having a sexual affair with a person not your spouse.

____ e. Refusing to give a tithe of your income to God and using it on yourself.

____ f. Participating in sexual relationships with family members who are not your spouse.

____ g. Taking unfair advantage of people to make more money for yourself.

____ h. Telling and listening to "dirty" jokes.

God is pure, holy, and righteous. All of the actions above are opposite to God's character. A person who practices these types of actions has given his heart to something other than God.

(Answers: S=d,f; I=b,c,h; G=a,e,g.)

© LifeWay Press, 1993. Used by Permission.

* You have permission to reproduce this worksheet from *Fresh Encounter Leader's Manual* for use in session 3 of your study of *God's Pattern for Revival and Spiritual Awakening.*

Television Family

© Lifeway Press 1993. Used by permission.
* You have permission to make an overhead cel from this sheet in *Fresh Encounter Leader's Manual* for use in session 3 of your study of *God's Pattern for Revival and Spiritual Awakening*.

Television Family

Show the picture of the family sitting around a television set.

Say: Suppose this is a typical family.

Describe the way they spend their time.

Describe their family life.

Describe their religious life.

Now show the picture of the Buddhist.

Buddhist

© Lifeway Press 1993. Used by permission.
* You have permission to make an overhead cel from this sheet in *Fresh Encounter Leader's Manual* for use in session 3 of your study of *God's Pattern for Revival and Spiritual Awakening*.

BUDDHIST

Show the picture of the Buddhist.

Say: Suppose this is a typical Buddhist. Though you may not know many details:

Describe the way he spends his time.

Describe his family life.

Describe his religious life.

COMPARE AND CONTRAST
Show the two pictures. Ask:
- In what ways are these people different in their love relationship with God?
- In what ways are these people similar in their love relationships with God?

Show the Buddhist. Ask:
What would this person need to do to move into a right love relationship with God?

Show the television family. Ask:
What changes do you think God might require of this family for them to have a faithful love relationship with Him?

Session 4: God Disciplines His People in Love

BEFORE THE SESSION

❏ 1. Study unit 4 of *God's Pattern for Revival and Spiritual Awakening* and complete the learning activities.
❏ 2. Pray for your group members during the week. Ask God to guide you as you prepare for this session. Ask God to prepare the hearts of His people for a fresh encounter with Him.
❏ 3. Read "During the Session" and allow the Holy Spirit to guide you as to which of the activities to use and how much time to devote to each. You may not have time to deal with all of these activities in one session.
❏ 4. Provide paper and pencils for the arrival activity or duplicate copies of the "Penalties for Disobedience" worksheet on LM page 103.
❏ 5. Provide copies of the "God Judged Judah" worksheet on LM page 102 or reproduce the following information on poster board.

GOD JUDGED JUDAH FOR ITS SIN

Israel departed from the Lord on many occasions. Because of the idolatry of Solomon in his later years, God divided the nation, taking ten tribes from under the rule of Solomon's son. In 721 B.C. the Northern Kingdom of Israel was destroyed by Assyria. In 586 B.C. God used Babylon to destroy Jerusalem and carry the people of the Southern Kingdom into captivity (the exile). God explained to the prophet Jeremiah what He had done.

Read Jeremiah 11:7-8 and answer the questions that follow:

> ⁷"'From the time I brought your forefathers up from Egypt until today, I warned them again and again, saying, "Obey me." ⁸But they did not listen or pay attention; instead, they followed the stubbornness of their evil hearts. So I brought on them all the curses of the covenant I had commanded them to follow but that they did not keep.'"

1. In verse 7, what did God ask from Israel?

2. How did the people respond to God's repeated warnings?

NOTES

3. How did God discipline them for their disobedience and rebellion? _____

> God wanted obedience from Israel. His first and foremost command was for them to love Him (Deut. 6:4-5). They had left the love relationship, and did not obey Him or keep the covenant relationship. They followed their own evil ways. So God kept His oath to bring about "curses" in His judgment. Notice He did not do this quickly. He spent hundreds of years trying to secure their obedience. This action was a final judgment.

❏ 6. Arrange the chairs in a semicircle facing a focal wall. Display the "God's Pattern" poster on the wall. Leave the key words for phases 1–2 in place on the diagram.

DURING THE SESSION

ARRIVAL ACTIVITY

1. **Greet members** as they arrive. Provide paper and pencils or the "Penalties for Disobedience" worksheet (LM p. 103) to half of the group members. Ask them to read Deuteronomy 28:15-48 and make a list of ways they sense God may be judging our nation.

    Give the other half of the members a copy of the "God Judged Judah" worksheet (LM p. 102). Ask these to complete it and be prepared to share a summary with the rest of the members.

2. **Opening Prayer.** Ask one of the group members to lead in an opening prayer asking for God's guidance to be revealed during the session.

3. **Report and Discuss.** Ask members to share the ways they think God may be bringing discipline on our nation. (For instance, one might say: "According to verses 43-44, aliens will grow in influence and the nation will become a debtor nation to aliens. I see reports where foreign interests are buying land, office buildings, and industries all across the country. Our uncontrollable national debt is another possible indicator that we are under God's discipline.")

    Ask members to think about nations that have fallen from power throughout history. Ask them to recall some of these judgments (from Deut. 28) that came upon those nations. You can include the biblical accounts of Israel, Judah, Assyria, Babylon, and Egypt.

    Call for a summary of the way God disciplined Judah for its sin.

GOD'S PATTERN

1. **Review Phases.** Call attention to the "God's Pattern" poster. Point to phases 1–2, one at a time, and ask for a volunteer to state each phase in his own words.

2. **Focus Phase of the Week.** Display the key words for phases 3–7 on the wall beside the poster or lay them on a table or the floor in front of the poster. Ask a volunteer to select the

key word for phase 3, place it on the poster, and state phase 3 in his own words.

CONTENT REVIEW

1. **Scripture Memory Verse.** Ask for a volunteer to quote Hebrews 12:5-6. Ask: What are three things God does to discipline His people?
2. **God's Nature.** Ask members to name as many words as possible that describe God's nature.
3. **Judgment.** Ask volunteers to define the following in their own words: "temporal judgment," "eternal judgment," "final judgment," and "remedial judgment."

    Ask members to think of a biblical example of each type of judgment.

    Ask members to turn to GP page 63. Ask volunteers to read the Scriptures and identify the truths they describe.
4. **Discipline.** Ask members to name a variety of ways God brings discipline on His people. Point out that the two terms *remedial judgment* and *discipline* are used interchangeably. Ask members not to get distracted by the use of terms. Allow questions or discussion if members seem to be confused or if they disagree with the terms used. Bring the group to an understanding of the truth that God does discipline His people.

    Ask: Why does God discipline His people? (Answer: Because He loves them, and He wants them to return to Him to experience fullness of life. God also wants them to return to His mission of reaching a lost world.)

ENCOUNTERING GOD

1. **Most Meaningful.** Ask members to turn to the unit review on GP page 68. Call on volunteers to share the statement, Scripture, or idea that was most meaningful to them. Encourage those who will to share their prayer response to God.
2. **What Is the Spirit Saying?** Ask: As you studied and prayed this week, what has God been saying to you about your life, your family, or our church?

DISCUSSION QUESTIONS

As time permits, guide members to discuss the following questions:

1. Why does God not take delight in the death of the wicked?
2. How is discipline a display of God's love?
3. Why do you think God brought final judgment on Ananias and Sapphira? (GP p. 62)
4. Why is God's discipline progressive—increasing in intensity?
5. How can a person know whether something bad is discipline from God?
6. How is the story of Job an illustration of the fact that bad things are not always judgment or discipline?
7. How could a Christian distinguish between godly discipline and spiritual warfare? How important is it to know the

difference? For instance, suppose a church assumed it was experiencing spiritual warfare when it was really being disciplined by God. What problems could that cause?
8. What is God saying to you through 2 Chronicles 15:2? (GP p. 66)
9. In your opinion, what was most meaningful or significant in the revival experienced under Asa and Azariah? (GP pp. 66–67)
10. In what ways, if any, do you sense our church is being (or has been) disciplined by God?

THE SECOND GREAT AWAKENING (GP P. 56)
Ask:
- What was your primary response to the report on the Second Great Awakening? Why?
- Did God use it to encourage, instruct, inspire, challenge, or convict you? How?
- How did the role of leadership affect the length of this awakening's impact on the nation?
- Why do you think this awakening had such an impact on missions?

CLEANSING BY WASHING WITH WATER THROUGH THE WORD
Ask members to turn to "Cleansing by Washing with Water Through the Word" on GP page 57.
1. **Wash Out.** Ask members to identify the things they marked that would be important to "wash out."
2. **Wash In.** Ask members to identify the things they marked that would be valuable to "wash in."
3. **Responding to God.** Ask: What, if anything, has God said to you through these Scriptures? How are you responding to Him?

PRAYER TRIPLETS
Ask prayer triplets to pray together about the following concerns:
1. **Petition for One Another.** Encourage members to share with their prayer triplets any area where they sense they or their family may be experiencing God's discipline. Take time to pray for each area of need that God might be victorious in those areas.
2. **Intercession for Our Church.** Ask triplets to pray for the leaders of your church. Pray for wisdom, courage, insight, and God's directions for these leaders.
3. **Prayer for the Nation.** Ask triplets to pray for our nation and its leaders. Ask God to reveal to them ways they may need to call our nation to repent and return to the Lord.
4. **Continue Praying.** Encourage prayer triplets to continue praying for each other during the coming week. Suggest that they get together during the week to pray.

AFTER THE SESSION

1. Make notes to yourself about your group members and ways you sense a need to pray for each of them. Do you sense that any of your members are clearly being disciplined by the Lord? Do you need to talk with them? This week, pray that God will reveal to members the meaning of repentance. Pray that God will help them be willing to repent in any areas they sense His conviction of sin.
2. Ask yourself the following questions and jot notes in the margin or on a separate sheet of paper.
   - What evidence did members give that they sensed God's discipline in:
     —their lives?
     —their families?
     —your church?
     —our nation?
   - Did members understand the fact that God's discipline is motivated by His love? Are any of them struggling with a sense of God's love?
   - Are any members suffering from God's discipline so severely that they need counseling or personal help? Whom should I contact about the matter? Or should I plan a personal visit?
   - Am I allowing enough time for prayer at the end of the session? Do I need to adjust the agenda for next week to allow more time for prayer? Should I start with prayer early in the session?
   - What spiritual or mental preparation do I need to make for the next session that may have been lacking this week?
   - Which of the members need to be encouraged to participate more in the sharing and discussion times? When and how will I encourage them?
   - When could I have responded more appropriately to the needs of members or to the leadership of the Holy Spirit?
3. Read "Before the Session" in the next session to get an idea of the preparation that will be required for your next group session.
4. Make a special note that the prayer time needs to be longer in the next session. Plan for adequate time for prayer.
5. Attend your leadership team meeting this week. Write down any concerns you may want to discuss during that meeting.

NOTES

God Judged Judah for Its Sin

Israel departed from the Lord on numerous occasions. Because of the idolatry of Solomon in his later years, God divided the nation taking 10 tribes from the rule of Solomon's son. In 721 B.C. the Northern Kingdom of Israel was destroyed by Assyria. In 586 B.C. God used Babylon to destroy Jerusalem and carry the people of the Southern Kingdom into captivity (the exile). God explained to the prophet Jeremiah what He had done.

Read Jeremiah 11:7-8 and answer the questions that follow.

JEREMIAH 11:7-8

⁷"From the time I brought your forefathers up from Egypt until today, I warned them again and again, saying, 'Obey me.' ⁸But they did not listen or pay attention; instead, they followed the stubbornness of their evil hearts. So I brought on them all the curses of the covenant I had commanded them to follow but that they did not keep."

1. In verse 7, what did God ask from Israel? _____

_____

2. How did the people respond to God's repeated warnings? _____

_____

3. How did God discipline them for their disobedience and rebellion? _____

_____

_____

God wanted obedience from Israel. God's first and foremost command was for the people of Israel to love Him (see Deut. 6:4-5). They had left the love relationship, and did not obey Him or keep the covenant relationship. They followed their own evil ways. So God kept His oath to bring about "curses" in His judgment. Notice that God did not do this quickly. God spent hundreds of years trying to secure their obedience. This action was a final judgment.

© LifeWay Press, 1993. Used by permission.

* You have permission to reproduce this worksheet from *Fresh Encounter Leader's Manual* for use in session 4 of your study of *God's Pattern for Revival and Spiritual Awakening*.

Scripture is from the Holy Bible, *New International Version*, copyright © 1973, 1978, 1984 by International Bible Society.

Penalties for Disobedience

Read these excerpts from Deuteronomy 28. Think about our nation, city, town, community, church, and families. If you see some similarities with your experience, place a check in the box beside them. If you do check some, go to the Lord and ask Him if you are being disciplined because of disobedience. If you are, God will let you know.

Deuteronomy 28

15If you do not obey the Lord your God and do not carefully follow all his commands and decrees I am giving you today, all these curses will come upon you and overtake you:

- ❑ 16You will be cursed in the city and cursed in the country.
- ❑ 18The fruit of your womb will be cursed, and the crops of your land.
- ❑ 20The Lord will send on you curses, confusion and rebuke in everything you put your hand to.
- ❑ 21The Lord will plague you with diseases.... 22with wasting disease, with fever and inflammation, with scorching heat and drought, with blight and mildew.
- ❑ 24The Lord will turn the rain of your country into dust and powder.
- ❑ 25The Lord will cause you to be defeated before your enemies. You will come at them from one direction but flee from them in seven.
- ❑ 28The Lord will afflict you with madness, blindness and confusion of mind.
- ❑ 29You will be unsuccessful in everything you do; day after day you will be oppressed and robbed, with no one to rescue you.
- ❑ 30You will be pledged to be married to a woman, but another will take her and ravish her.
- ❑ 32Your sons and daughters will be given to another nation, and you will wear out your eyes watching for them day after day, powerless to lift a hand.
- ❑ 34The sights you see will drive you mad.
- ❑ 38You will sow much seed in the field but you will harvest little.
- ❑ 43The alien who lives among you will rise above you higher and higher, but you will sink lower and lower.
- ❑ 44He will lend to you, but you will not lend to him. He will be the head, but you will be the tail.
- ❑ 65The Lord will give you an anxious mind, eyes weary with longing, and a despairing heart. 66You will live in constant suspense, filled with dread both night and day, never sure of your life. 67In the morning you will say, "If only it were evening!" and in the evening, "If only it were morning!"—because of the terror that will fill your hearts and the sights that your eyes will see.

45All these curses will come upon you. They will pursue you and overtake you until you are destroyed, because you did not obey the Lord your God and observe the commands and decrees he gave you. 46They will be a sign and a wonder to you and your descendants forever. 47Because you did not serve the Lord your God joyfully and gladly in the time of prosperity, 48 therefore in hunger and thirst, in nakedness and dire poverty, you will serve the enemies the Lord sends against you.

63Just as it pleased the Lord to make you prosper and increase in number, so it will please him to ruin and destroy you.

© LifeWay Press, 1993. Used by Permission.

* You have permission to reproduce this worksheet from *Fresh Encounter Leader's manual* for use in session 4 of your study of *God's Pattern for Revival and Spiritual Awakening*.

Scripture is from the Holy Bible, *New International Version*, copyright © 1973, 1978, 1984 by International Bible Society.

Session 5: God Calls His People to Repent

BEFORE THE SESSION

❏ 1. Study Unit 5 of *God's Pattern for Revival and Spiritual Awakening* and complete the learning activities.
❏ 2. Pray for your group members during the week. Ask God to guide you as you prepare for this session. Ask God to prepare the hearts of His people for a fresh encounter with Him.
❏ 3. Read "During the Session" and allow the Holy Spirit to guide you as to which of the activities to use and how much time to devote to each. You may not have time to deal with all of these activities in one session.
❏ 4. Provide copies of the "Your First Love" worksheet (LM p. 109) for members or copy the following on poster board.

YOUR FIRST LOVE

MARK 12:28-30 • ²⁸One of the teachers of the law came and . . . asked [Jesus], "Of all the commandments, which is the most important?"
²⁹"The most important one," answered Jesus, "is this: 'Hear, O Israel, the Lord our God, the Lord is one. ³⁰Love the Lord your God with all your heart and with all your soul and with all your mind and with all your strength.' "

1. Which of the following best describes God's greatest desire for His people?
   a. God wants His people to lead others to faith in His Son Jesus.
   b. God wants His people to love Him with their total beings.
   c. God wants His people to give generously to His kingdom's work.
   d. God wants His people to love one another and display unity.
2. Can you describe your love for God by claiming sincerely, "I love you with all my heart, soul, mind, and strength"?
   ❏ Yes   ❏ No

RETURN TO YOUR FIRST LOVE

REVELATION 2:1-5 • ¹"To the angel of the church in Ephesus write: . . . ²I know your deeds, your hard work and your

> perseverance. I know that you cannot tolerate wicked men, that you have tested those who claim to be apostles but are not, and have found them false. ³You have persevered and have endured hardships for my name, and have not grown weary.
>
> ⁴Yet I hold this against you: You have forsaken your first love. ⁵Remember the height from which you have fallen! Repent and do the things you did at first. If you do not repent, I will come to you and remove your lampstand from its place."
>
> 1. For what did Jesus commend the church at Ephesus? (vv. 2–3) _____
>
> 2. Check the response that best describes the way Jesus viewed the church.
>   ❏ a. They had forsaken their first love, but their good works balanced out the bad. Everything is okay.
>   ❏ b. They had forsaken their first love, and they must repent and return to their first love or be removed.
>
> 3. Pray and ask God about the quality of your love relationship with Him. Do you sense a need to return to your first love individually? as a family? as a church? as a denomination?

❏ 5. Notice that the prayer activity for prayer triplets may require more time than usual. Be sure to allow sufficient time at the end for this.

❏ 6. Arrange the chairs in a semicircle facing a focal wall. Display the "God's Pattern" poster on the wall. Leave the key words for phases 1–3 in place on the diagram.

Note: During this session, some members may struggle with the use of the word *perish* in regard to a believer. After all, John 3:16 says that "whoever believes in him shall not perish." In John 10:27-28, Jesus said, "My sheep listen to my voice; I know them, and they follow me. I give them eternal life, and they shall never perish." Remind group members that the context in this discussion is temporal judgment, not eternal life (GP, p. 60). The Greek word translated "perish" (Middle Voice) is also translated "destroy." The New Testament examples of Ananias and Sapphira (Acts 5:1-5), the Corinthian believers who were sick or dead (1 Cor. 11:17-34), and the promised removal of an unrepentant Ephesian church (Rev. 2:5) all describe believers and a church who perished. This did not influence their eternal destiny, but they did experience ruin and loss. They were destroyed. Unrepentant believers are of no use to God for His kingdom purposes. There are consequences for believers who refuse to repent of known sin. Help members understand the meaning of this word if its use raises questions.

NOTES

DURING THE SESSION

ARRIVAL ACTIVITY
1. **Greet members** as they arrive. Distribute copies of the "Your First Love" worksheet (LM p. 109) and ask members to complete it.
2. **Opening Prayer.** Ask groups of four or five to go to the Lord in prayer. Encourage as many as will to pray in each group.
3. **What Is the Spirit Saying?** Remain in groups of four or five. Ask members in each group to turn to the unit review on GP page 82 and to share the statement, Scripture, or idea that was most meaningful to them. Encourage those who will to share their prayer response to God.

    Call members back into the larger group. Ask: As you studied and prayed this week, what has God been saying to you about your life, your family, or our church?

GOD'S PATTERN
1. **Review Phases.** Call attention to the poster. Point to phases 1–3, one at a time, and ask for a volunteer to state each phase in her own words.
2. **Focus Phases of the Week.** Display the key words for phases 4–7 on the wall beside the poster or lay them on a table or the floor in front of the poster. Ask a volunteer to select the key word for phase 4, place it on the poster, and state phase 4 in his own words. Do the same for phase 5.

CONTENT REVIEW
1. **Scripture Memory Verse.** Ask for a volunteer to quote Malachi 3:7.
2. **Requirements for Revival.** Ask a volunteer to name the four requirements for revival mentioned in 2 Chronicles 7:14.
3. **Symptoms.** Ask members to describe at least three symptoms or signs of spiritual sickness. (Answer: God's discipline, substitutes for God, and disobedience) Ask: What do these three symptoms indicate as the root problem? (Answer: a heart shift; something is wrong with the love relationship with God)
4. **Repent.** Ask a volunteer to define "repent" in his own words. Allow others to elaborate on the definition or add to it. Ask: What are three changes required in repentance? (Answer: Change of mind, heart, and will)

DISCUSSION QUESTIONS
As time permits, guide members to discuss the following questions:
1. What is the best evidence that repentance has taken place? Why?
2. What happens to God's people who refuse to repent?
3. What statement or experience in the revival under Josiah and Hilkiah seems most significant to you?
4. What significance do you see in the order of events in this revival? (GP, p. 79)
5. What are some things for which a church might need to repent?

6. How can (does) a church repent?

THE PRAYER REVIVAL OF 1857–58 (GP, P. 70)
Ask:
- What was your response to the report on the Prayer Revival of 1857–58? Why?
- Did God use it to encourage, instruct, inspire, challenge, or convict you? How?
- What affect did financial disaster have on the beginning of the revival? How would people respond today with a similar disaster?
- What was the relationship of prayer to the beginning of the revival?

CLEANSING BY WASHING WITH WATER THROUGH THE WORD
Ask members to turn to "Cleansing by Washing with Water Through the Word" on GP page 71.
1. **Wash Out.** Ask members to identify the things they marked that would be important to "wash out."
2. **Wash In.** Ask members to identify the things they marked that would be valuable to "wash in."
3. **Responding to God.** Ask: What, if anything, has God said to you through these Scriptures? How are you responding?

PRAYER TRIPLETS
Ask prayer triplets to pray together about the following concerns. You should not interrupt this time of prayer, so announce that groups should dismiss themselves after they complete their prayer times.

1. **Petition for One Another.** Read James 5:13-20. A good guideline for confession is: "Confession of sin should be limited to the circle of offense" (T. W. Hunt in *Disciple's Prayer Life*, p. 133). Mutual confession, like that suggested in James 5:16, may be helpful for sin-weaknesses or besetting habits. "Public confession . . . should never endanger anyone else's privacy or reputation" (Hunt, p. 132).

    Suggest that triplets may want to follow the Holy Spirit's prompting and confess sins to one another, pray for one another, and be healed. Encourage them to respond to the Spirit's prompting and not to any other pressures.
2. **Intercession for Our Church.** Ask triplets to confess and seek forgiveness for anything they sense your church has done for which repentance would be required. Pray for the Holy Spirit to bring conviction of sin to other church members and leaders if these are indeed areas for which repentance is required. Pray that your pastor and other key leaders will provide sound spiritual leadership like Josiah did anytime your church needs to turn to the Lord.
3. **Continue Praying.** Encourage prayer triplets to continue praying for each other during the coming week. Suggest that they get together during the week to pray.

NOTES

AFTER THE SESSION

1. Make notes to yourself about your group members and ways you sense a need to pray for each of them. This week, pray that members will repent of any known sin and begin to experience God's cleansing and revival.
2. Ask yourself the following questions and jot notes in the margin or on a separate sheet of paper.
   - Which members (if any) are having problems with their love relationship with God? Which have an obedience problem that became evident during the session? How should I respond to help them?
   - Did any confessions surface in the session that need to be shared with the larger church body? (If so, you may want to call the member involved and suggest it if you have not already done so.)
   - Are any group members carrying a special burden for our church? Should I encourage them to get with other like-minded people to pray?
   - What spiritual or mental preparation do I need to make for the next session that may have been lacking this week?
   - Which of the members need to be encouraged to participate more in the sharing and discussion times? When and how will I encourage them?
   - When could I have responded more appropriately to the needs of members or to the leadership of the Holy Spirit?
3. Read "Before the Session" on the following page to get an idea of the preparation that will be required for your next group session.
4. Attend your leadership team meeting this week. Write down any concerns you may want to discuss during that meeting.

Your First Love

MARK 12:28-30

²⁸One of the teachers of the law came and . . . asked him [Jesus], "Of all the commandments, which is the most important?"

²⁹"The most important one," answered Jesus, "is this: 'Hear, O Israel, the Lord our God, the Lord is one. ³⁰Love the Lord your God with all your heart and with all your soul and with all your mind and with all your strength.' "

1. Which of the following best describes God's greatest desire for His people? Check one.
   - ❏ a. God wants His people to lead others to faith in His Son Jesus.
   - ❏ b. God wants His people to love Him with their total beings.
   - ❏ c. God wants His people to give generously to His kingdom's work.
   - ❏ d. God wants His people to love one another and display unity.

2. Can you describe your love for God by claiming sincerely, "I love you with all my heart, soul, mind, and strength"?   ❏ Yes   ❏ No

RETURN TO YOUR FIRST LOVE

REVELATION 2:1-5

¹"To the angel of the church in Ephesus write: . . . ²I know your deeds, your hard work and your perseverance. I know that you cannot tolerate wicked men, that you have tested those who claim to be apostles but are not, and have found them false. ³You have persevered and have endured hardships for my name, and have not grown weary.

⁴Yet I hold this against you: You have forsaken your first love. ⁵Remember the height from which you have fallen! Repent and do the things you did at first. If you do not repent, I will come to you and remove your lampstand from its place."

1. For what did Jesus commend the church at Ephesus?
   _____
   _____
   _____

2. Check below the way Jesus viewed the church.
   - ❏ a. They had forsaken their first love, but their good works balanced out the bad. Everything is okay.
   - ❏ b. They had forsaken their first love, and they must repent and return to their first love or be removed.

3. Pray and ask God about the quality of your love relationship with Him. Do you sense a need to return to your first love individually? as a family? as a church? as a denomination?

© LifeWay Press, 1993. Used by Permission.
* You have permission to reproduce this worksheet from *Fresh Encounter Leader's Manual* for use in session 5 of your study of *God's Pattern for Revival and Spiritual Awakening.*

Scripture is from the Holy Bible, *New International Version*, copyright © 1973, 1978, 1984 by International Bible Society.

NOTES

Session 6: God Revives His Repentant People

BEFORE THE SESSION

❏ 1. Study Unit 6 of *God's Pattern for Revival and Spiritual Awakening* and complete the learning activities.
❏ 2. Pray for your group members during the week. Ask God to guide you as you prepare for this session. Ask God to prepare the hearts of His people for a fresh encounter with Him.
❏ 3. Read "During the Session" and allow the Holy Spirit to guide you as to which of the activities to use and how much time to devote to each. You may not have time to deal with all of these activities in one session.
❏ 4. Write the following Scripture references on a chalkboard or poster for the arrival activity: Psalm 30:4-12; Psalm 94:19; Psalm 126:5-6; Psalm 147:3; Isaiah 61:1-4; Ezekiel 36:26; Matthew 11:28-30; 2 Corinthians 7:5-6; 2 Corinthians 12:9-10.
❏ 5. Make one copy of the "Asbury Revival Testimonies" (LM pp. 116–117) and cut them apart for distribution.
❏ 6. Arrange the chairs in a semicircle facing a focal wall. Display the "God's Pattern" poster on the wall. Leave the key words for phases 1–5 in place on the diagram.

DURING THE SESSION

ARRIVAL ACTIVITY

1. **Greet members** as they arrive. Ask members to read the Scriptures you have written on the chalkboard or poster and to list divine exchanges—combinations of things God removes and replaces. For example, God says He will take away our stone heart and replace it with a heart of flesh.
   While they are working, enlist seven people to read the "Asbury Revival Testimonies."
2. **Reports.** Ask members to share what they discovered. See if they can think of any other divine exchanges like: forgiveness for guilt. You may want to suggest that a member prepare an attractive poster listing "Divine Exchanges." Here are some divine exchanges they may have found:

- rejoicing for weeping
- wailing into dancing
- joy for sackcloth (mourning)
- singing heart for silence
- rest for the weary
- freedom for the captives
- comfort for mourning
- consolation for anxiety
- songs of joy for tears
- joy for weeping
- healing to the brokenhearted
- heart of flesh for heart of stone
- new spirit for old spirit
- comfort for the downcast

- crown of beauty for ashes
- ruins rebuilt
- devastated cities renewed
- oil of gladness for spirit of despair
- devastated cities restored

Some other divine exchanges mentioned in Scripture include:

- forgiveness for guilt
- strength for weakness
- water to the thirsty
- justice for the oppressed
- cure for backsliding
- families for the lonely
- life for death
- peace for anxiety
- righteousness for unrighteousness
- streams of water for the desert
- bread for the hungry
- light for darkness
- guidance for disoriented
- refuge for the distressed
- boldness and confidence for fear
- shepherds for the sheep without a shepherd

3. **Opening Prayer.** Ask members to pray sentence prayers thanking God for His divine exchanges. Close this prayer time asking for God's continued work in bringing revival to your church, city, and nation.

GOD'S PATTERN
1. **Review Phases.** Call attention to the poster. Point to phases 1–5, one at a time, and ask for a volunteer to state each phase in his own words.
2. **Focus Phases of the Week.** Display the key words for phases 6–7 on the wall beside the poster or lay them on a table or the floor in front of the poster. Ask a volunteer to select the key word for phase 6, place it on the poster, and state phase 6 in her own words. Do the same for phase 7.

CONTENT REVIEW
1. **Scripture Memory Verse.** Ask for a volunteer to quote Ephesians 3:20-21.
2. **Role of Prayer.** Ask a member to explain the role of prayer in revival. Make sure the emphasis is placed on the connection between prayer and repentance.
3. **Revival.** Ask a volunteer to define revival in his own words. Ask members to turn to GP pages 88–89 and list the signs they found that revival had taken place under Hezekiah's leadership.
4. **God's Work.** Ask the group to mention things God does when He brings revival.

ENCOUNTERING GOD
1. **Most Meaningful.** Ask members to turn to the unit review on GP page 96. Call for volunteers to share the statement, Scripture, or idea that was most meaningful to them. Encourage those who will to share their prayer response to God.
2. **What Is the Spirit Saying?** Ask: As you studied and prayed this week, what has God been saying to you about your life, family, or our church?

NOTES

3. **Review of the Study.** Ask members to share their responses to item 9 on GP page 96: What is the most important thing you sense God has said to you during this study? In your opinion, what is the most important thing God is saying to our church? our city? our nation?

DISCUSSION QUESTIONS
As time permits, guide members to discuss the following questions:
1. How is God's glory evident through the church? (GP p. 86)
2. How is our church carrying out the ministry of reconciliation?
3. How should we respond to people in our church who scorn and ridicule a call to revival like the people of Hezekiah's day?
4. Ask members to turn to GP page 91 and review the factors common to corporate revival experiences. Ask: Which of these factors was most meaningful to recognize? most encouraging?
5. What are some of the greatest barriers to revival?
6. J. Edwin Orr said, "Revival is like judgment day." What are some aspects of the revival process that are difficult for individuals and churches?
7. What are the benefits of going through God's revival process?
8. How can we know when revival has taken place?
9. What are some ways we can do a better job of praying for revival individually and as a church?
10. What are some ways a church can prepare for the coming of the Lord in revival and awakening?

THE ASBURY REVIVAL (GP P. 84)
1. **Testimonies.** Ask enlisted members to read their assigned testimonies.

   Editor of the Student Newspaper. "I knew things in my life were a lie. I was a National Merit Scholar and a real 'campus leader.' A lot of good they were doing me because I was sick and a miserably lonely young man. Yet I sat there for two hours refusing to do anything about it. A girl on my staff came up and hugged me around the neck and apologized for 'being mean' to me. That really got me, because it was I who had mistreated her!

   "As I watched and listened to my fellow students, I was troubled to realize I lacked a certain joy and happiness that so many of them expressed so freely. There came that critical moment when I was forced to admit that my self-sufficiency was failing me and that I needed to be dependent upon Jesus Christ."

   A Senior Premedical Student. "I have been a Christian for nearly ten years, but the real freedom to express myself was never a reality in my life. "I guess the problem was a matter of not really having accepted the forgiveness of God for the sins which I had committed. God had forgiven me all right but I had never forgiven myself.

"For years, then, I suffered under the awful burden of self-imposed, false guilt. I continually berated myself for not living up to the way of God. . . . Because of this inner restlessness I was unable in all of those years to give a meaningful verbal witness to my faith in Jesus Christ. . . .

"Late one night in the balcony of Hughes Auditorium, feeling so worthless watching everyone come alive in the spirit of the revival, I poured out the distress of my heart to a friend. With love and understanding he helped me to see that I had been falsely punishing myself for all of these years.

"My heart began to beat with a fresh thrill as I saw that indeed God's forgiveness had afforded peace to me years before. I prayed then and with joy and triumph. That seat in the balcony became a hallowed place of prayer. . . .

"From the very first weekend of the revival Christ has been able to use me. That weekend in my home church two dozen people responded to an invitation to the altar after I had given my testimony. It was a new thrill to have been used of God for the first time in my life. Since then I have seized upon every chance to bear witness to my newly understood faith. I have seen hundreds of people come to know Jesus Christ."

Young Wife. "I was born and reared in a preacher's home. Now I am married to a preacher. I've gone to church all of my life just because it was the thing to do. But it has never meant much to me. Now I know why. I've just asked Jesus to come into my heart, and He has."

A College Basketball Coach. "I have not been the Christian witness I should have been in front of the men on the team. I have failed them as a Christian. I want God to forgive me. I am a different person."

Son of a Well-Known Preacher. (He had heard thousands of sermons on the subject of salvation, but had never been saved himself.) "For years I had everybody fooled, but I never really fooled myself because God gave me no peace. Now He has met the longing of my heart."

A Psychology Professor. (He brokenheartedly confessed that he had been living a sham for six years.) "I have been keeping up the outward appearances, but there has been no peace or joy in my life. It has been dry. I can't go on like this." Two days later: "God has given me a new joy in my life, a new purpose for living."

A Witness. "For every prayer He answered, He gave me two more burdens. You should see my prayer list now."

These first person testimonies are from *One Divine Moment: The Asbury Revival* edited by Robert E. Coleman, Old Tappan: Fleming H. Revell Company, 1970.

2. **Response.** Ask:
   - What was your primary response to the report on the Asbury Revival? Why?
   - Did God use it to encourage, instruct, inspire, challenge, or convict you? How?
   - How did the sharing of testimonies contribute to the spread of the revival?
   - Why did the revival have such a powerful beginning and such a short life?
3. **Application.** Discuss one or more of the following questions:
   - Why do you think personal or "eye witness" testimonies of revival have such an impact on the spread of revival?
   - What times in your church life do members have opportunity to share with others what God is doing in their lives? If testimonies are not encouraged in your church, when do you think would be good times for testimonies?

CLEANSING BY WASHING WITH WATER THROUGH THE WORD

Ask members to turn to "Cleansing by Washing with Water Through the Word" on GP page 85.
1. **Wash Out.** Ask members to identify the things they marked that would be important to "wash out."
2. **Wash In.** Ask members to identify the things they marked that would be valuable to "wash in."
3. **Responding to God.** Ask: What, if anything, has God said to you through these Scriptures? How are you responding to Him?

PRAYER TRIPLETS

Ask prayer triplets to pray together about the following concerns:
1. **Petition for One Another.** Ask members to turn to GP page 95 and review what they may have marked in the "Encountering God in Prayer" activity. Encourage each member to share one or more areas in which the others could pray for him. Then allow the triplets to pray for each other.
2. **Intercession for Our Church.** Ask members to pray for your pastor and church leaders as they seek God's directions about leading you through *A Plumb Line for God's People*.
3. **Continue Praying.** Encourage prayer triplets to consider praying together during the coming weeks. Suggest that they may want to get together each week to pray for each other, your church, lost people in the community, your city, and the nation.

CLOSING

1. **A Plumb Line.** Share with the group what plans have been made for the use of *A Plumb Line for God's People* in the corporate worship setting of your church. Encourage members to continue praying for your pastor and other church leaders as they guide members to respond to God.

2. **Thanks.** Take a moment to thank members for their preparation and participation in the study.
3. **Closing Prayer.** Stand and join hands in a circle. Ask members who will to pray brief prayers responding to what God has been saying and doing during your study together.

AFTER THE SESSION

1. Add to your prayer list or journal a list of specific ways you sense a need to continue praying for group members or for your church.
2. Ask yourself the following questions and jot notes in the margin or on a separate sheet of paper.
   - What are some of the most important things members sensed God said to them during the study?
   - What (if anything) seems to be a barrier to revival in my church or community?
   - What evidence do I see that God is bringing revival to individuals in my group? in my church?
   - Which members of my group (if any) have personal testimonies that need to be shared with my church? Who should I tell? When could the testimonies be shared?
   - Did any confessions surface in the session that really need to be shared with the larger church body? (If so, you may want to call the member involved and suggest it if you have not already done so.)
   - Do I sense that we need further study on God's pattern? Should we plan for a review in the near future? How soon?
   - What unresolved problems do I need to handle?
   - What issues have surfaced that need to be addressed by the church leaders?
3. Save the "God's Pattern" poster, all diagrams, and other leadership resources that may be needed in a future study of *God's Pattern for Revival and Spiritual Awakening*.
4. Attend your leadership team meeting this week for a final evaluation of the study. Write down any concerns you may want to discuss during that meeting.

N O T E S

Asbury Revival Testimonies

Editor of the Student Newspaper. "I knew things in my life were a lie. I was a National Merit Scholar and a real 'campus leader.' A lot of good they were doing me because I was sick and a miserably lonely young man. Yet I sat there for two hours refusing to do anything about it. A girl on my staff came up and hugged me around the neck and apologized for 'being mean' to me. That really got me, because it was I who had mistreated her!

"As I watched and listened to my fellow students, I was troubled to realize I lacked a certain joy and happiness that so many of them expressed so freely. There came that critical moment when I was forced to admit that my self-sufficiency was failing me and that I needed to be dependent upon Jesus Christ."

A Senior Premedical Student. "I had been a Christian for nearly ten years, but the real freedom to express myself was never a reality in my life. I guess the problem was a matter of not really having accepted the forgiveness of God for the sins which I had committed. God had forgiven me all right but I had never forgiven myself.

"For years, then, I suffered under the awful burden of self-imposed, false guilt. I continually berated myself for not living up to the way of God. . . . Because of this inner restlessness I was unable in all of those years to give a meaningful verbal witness to my faith in Jesus Christ. . . .

"Late one night in the balcony of Hughes Auditorium, feeling so worthless watching everyone come alive in the spirit of the revival, I poured out the distress of my heart to a friend. With love and understanding he helped me to see that I had been falsely punishing myself for all of these years.

"My heart began to beat with a fresh thrill as I saw that indeed God's forgiveness had afforded peace to me years before. I prayed then with joy and triumph. That seat in the balcony became a hallowed place of prayer. . . .

"From the very first weekend of the revival Christ has been able to use me. That weekend in my home church two dozen people responded to an invitation to the altar after I had given my testimony. It was a new thrill to have been used of God for the first time in my life. Since then I have seized upon every chance to bear witness to my newly understood faith. I have seen hundreds of people come to know Jesus Christ."

Young Wife. "I was born and reared in a preacher's home. Now I am married to a preacher. I've gone to church all of my life just because it was the thing to do. But it has never meant much to me. Now I know why. I've just asked Jesus to come into my heart, and He has."

A College Basketball Coach. "I have not been the Christian witness I should have been in front of the men on the team. I have failed them as a Christian. I want God to forgive me. I am a different person."

Son of a Well-Known Preacher. (He had heard thousands of sermons on the subject of salvation, but had never been saved himself.) "For years I had everybody fooled, but I never really fooled myself because God gave me no peace. Now He has met the longing of my heart."

A Psychology Professor. (He brokenheartedly confessed that he had been living a sham for six years.) "I have been keeping up the outward appearances, but there has been no peace or joy in my life. It has been dry. I can't go on like this." Two days later: "God has given me a new joy in my life, a new purpose for living."

A Witness. "For every prayer He answered, He gave me two more burdens. You should see my prayer list now."

These first person testimonies are from *One Divine Moment: The Asbury Revival* edited by Robert E. Coleman, Old Tappan: Fleming H. Revell Company, 1970; 38, 46–48, 58, 62–63.

© LifeWay Press, 1993. Used by permission.
* You have permission to reproduce these testimonies from *Fresh Encounter Leader's Manual* for use in session 6 of your study of *God's Pattern for Revival and Spiritual Awakening.*